FENCED OUT, FENCED IN

BORDER PROTECTION, ASYLUM AND DETENTION IN AUSTRALIA

EDITED BY
NATALIE BOLZAN, MICHAEL DARCY AND JAN MASON

FENCED OUT, FENCED IN

BORDER PROTECTION, ASYLUM AND DETENTION IN AUSTRALIA

EDITED BY

NATALIE BOLZAN, MICHAEL DARCY AND JAN MASON

University of
Western Sydney

COMMON
GROUND

S J S C
Research Centre

This book is published at theHumanities.com
a series imprint of theUniversityPress.com

First published in Australia in 2006 by
Common Ground Publishing Pty Ltd
PO Box 463
Altona Vic 3018
ABN 66 074 822 629
www.theHumanities.com

National Library of Australia Cataloguing-in-Publication data:

Fenced Out, Fenced In: Border Protection, Asylum and Detention in Australia.

Bibliography.
ISBN 1 86335 599 5

1. Illegal aliens Australia - Anecdotes. 2. Asylum, Right of - Australia. 3. Alien detention centers - Australia. 4. Illegal aliens - Government policy - Australia. I. Bolzan, Natalie. II. Darcy, Michael.III. Mason, Jan.

325.210994

Cover designed by Diana Kalantzis
Cover image by project x graphics
Typeset in Australia by Common Ground Publishing.
Printed in Australia by Mercury on 80gsm Offset.

CONTENTS

CONTRIBUTORS

Natalie Bolzan is an Associate Professor in Social Work and the University of Western Sydney. As a member of the Social Justice Social Change Research Centre her research and writing focuses on exploring the ways marginalised groups challenge their marginalised status she is involved in research which enables marginalised or disadvantaged individuals or groups to have voice and to contribute to decisions which affect them.

Michael Darcy, at the time of publication, is an Associate Professor and Acting Director of the Social Justice and Social Change Research Centre at UWS. His research focuses, amongst other things, on the way in which local and community issues are constructed in policy discourse.

Jan Mason is Professor of Social Work and a member of the Social Justice and Social Change Research Centre at the University of Western Sydney. She researches broadly in the area of social work as well as specifically in child welfare and children's issues, with a particular focus on engaging children and young people in contributing to research and policies which concern them.

Judy Cashmore is President of Defence for Children (Australia) and a member of the Board of the National Children's and Youth Law Centre.

Mary Crock is an Associate Professor and Associate Dean, Postgraduate Research in the Faculty of Law, University of Sydney. She is an accredited specialist in immigration law; has written many books and articles on immigration and refugee law and is well known as an advocate and researcher in this area.

Fran Gale is Research Fellow in the Social Justice Social Change Research Centre, at the University of Western Sydney. One focus of her work is with marginalized young people from diverse and often traumatized populations, she has worked with asylum seekers and is involved in research concerning the mental health of asylum seekers.

Chris Sidoti is Director of the International Service for Human Rights based in Geneva. He is also Adjunct Professor at three Australian universities, the University of Western Sydney, the Australian Catholic University and Griffith University. He has been Australian Human Rights Commissioner (1995-2000) and Australian Law Reform Commissioner (1992 to 1995)

Jacqueline Everitt is a human rights lawyer, who works with the Edmund Rice Centre on refugee and children's rights. She worked with Maurice Blackman Cashman Solicitors to take the case of Iranian child refugee, Shayan Badraie, to the Supreme Court of NSW in a compensation claim for damages caused by his detention in Woomera IDPC and Villawood IDC. The first case of its kind, the case settled before judgment for $400,000 compensation plus costs to the child.

Michael Head teaches law at the University of Western Sydney, specialising in civil liberties, public law and socialist legal theory. He is author of Administrative Law: Context and Critique, Federation Press 2005, and (with Dr Scott Mann) Law in Perspective: Critical Thinking, Ethics and Society, UNSW Press 2005.

ACKNOWLEDGEMENTS

We wish to acknowledge the bravery, valour and generosity of the young refugees whose stories are told in this volume, as well as the sadness and despair they, their families and the many others who sought and still seek asylum in Australia experience at the hands of an unjust and inhumane Australian system.

The efforts of the contributors to this book, in writing about the plight of refugees, place them in solidarity with asylum seekers; we value their ongoing work to fully illuminate the injustice, inhumanity and callousness of current refugee policies. The work of Samia Michail and Claire Sidoti in painstakingly reviewing this work has meant that the implications of current refuges policies can be understood at the broader level of its impacts on all Australians and we thank then for their conscientiousness in assisting in this work.

We wish to acknowledge the support, for the conduct of one of the seminars at which many of the contributions to this book were first presented, provided by Defence for Children International (Australia) and the Association of Child Welfare Agencies (ACWA). Finally we want to thank the young Australians whose honesty and thoughtfulness yet again has made us stop and ask, 'what are we doing to ourselves?'.

LIST OF ACRONYMS

ABC	Australian Broadcasting Corporation
ACM	Australian Correctional Management
ALP	Australian Labour Party
DIMIA	Department of Immigration and Indigenous Affairs
DoCs	Department of Community Services
HREOC	Human Rights and Equal Opportunity Commission
IDC	Immigration Detention Centre
IOM	International Organisation for Migration
PNG	Papua New Guinea
PTSD	Post Traumatic Distress Disorder
RRT	Refugee Review Tribunal
SIEV	Suspected Illegal Entry Vessel
SUNC	Suspected Unlawful Citizen
UAM	Unaccompanied Minor
UN	United Nations
UNCLOS	United Nations Convention in the Rights of the Sea
UNHCR	United Nations High Commission for Refugees
UWS	University of Western Sydney

INTRODUCTION

HEARING THE VOICES OF ASYLUM SEEKERS

A CHALLENGE TO OUR HUMANITY

NATALIE BOLZAN AND JAN MASON

In August 2001, 438 people onboard the Norwegian freighter the Tampa, sought asylum in Australia. The Australian response was swift, consistent and hard line. These asylum seekers were not welcome in Australia. The Government argued their position by claiming these people were undeserving, unfit and untrustworthy. The asylum seekers were described as attempting to 'manipulate an immigration outcome' by claiming asylum and queue jumping rather than waiting their turn for orderly processing. They were suspected as 'would be' terrorists, seeking entry to an unsuspecting, innocent and possibly too generous country. Most graphically, and with apparent photographic evidence, they were constructed by the Government as people who would throw their babies overboard in order to hold a decent country to ransom. A story emerged, loud and clear, about these 'Others' who were not fit to live amongst us. Their very attempt to seek refuge in Australia was constructed as a threat to Australia's sovereign right to determine who lives here (Burke, 2001; Allard, 2001; Cock & Ludlow, 2001; Douez & Forbes, 2001; Allard & Clennell, 2001).

Whereas those constructing the demonizing of asylum seekers had wide coverage of their claims, asylum seekers were offered no opportunity to challenge these demonising constructions. To add insult to injury every effort made by the people held in detention to bring attention to their plight was discounted and cited as further evidence of their 'unfitness' to live amongst us. The drastic gesture of sewing lips together and fasting was constructed as a barbaric people stitching their children's lips in a cruel and inhuman gesture (Ahwan, 2002; Taylor, 2002; Madigan, Dunn & Buttler, 2002). The Government discussed protests in the desert detention centre at Woomera as riots of unruly mobs unable to conduct themselves in a civilised manner, of people who were unwilling to observe due process. The Government's spin on the situation of asylum seekers dominated the discourse around them and provided no opportunity to challenge this construction. Since the time of the Tampa asylum seekers several books have been written (Marr & Wilkinson, 2003; Weller, 2002; Kevin, 2004) describing in detail what occurred and trying to make sense of policies which set Australia in contravention of United Nations conventions, challenged international law and appeared to reverse previous humanitarian policies toward asylum seekers. Such works contribute to an overall understanding of not only what happened around the Tampa incident, but also its meaning both at the time and for today.

In beginning this book, we too were attempting to deal with the silencing of the many voices affected by the situation of the Tampa refugees and those who followed them. Amongst these voices are those of the young people who were incarcerated in the Australian detention centres and of people who had been able to gain access to these centres and could describe what was going on behind the barbed wire. During the process of compiling this book and bringing these voices together, we became aware of a greater silence surrounding the Australian response to refugees. The unasked and unanswered questions which emerged from labeling refugees as 'unworthy others' were concerned with 'who then are we?'

This current volume seeks to add to the process of trying to understand and make meaning by providing insights from the perspective of people who would challenge the Government's construction of the 'problem of asylum seekers' and question the distinctions between 'us' and 'them'. It is an opportunity to hear some of the voices absent from the forums where policies concerning asylum seekers were made. We take the sewing together of lips as a metaphor for the silencing, not only of a people and those who would stand with them, but of the whole country affected by the decisions made by those in government. The essays presented here expose us to the constructions, most notably from asylum seekers themselves but also from others, of people who have a contrary position and understanding to that of the government. This book is an outcome of two seminars held at the University of Western Sydney (UWS) designed to provide spaces for listening to voices, alternative to those dominant in public forums and the media. The first seminar, organised by the Social Justice and

Social Change Research Centre, was convened to inform ourselves and other persons and organisations interested in contributing to the Human Rights and Equal Opportunity Commission inquiry about the issues around children and families in immigration detention centres. The second seminar was organised by Michael Head from the School of Law at UWS to discuss the Government's hurried legislative response to these issues.

Beyond this, the current volume asks what type of country are we creating when the voices of the marginalised, the dispossessed and the disadvantaged are utterly absent from debates concerning them? In fencing asylum seekers out of our country in the way we have, what kind of country have we created for those who, by default, have become fenced in?

We begin this book with the voices of young people who fled their homelands. These young people did not flee for economic gain, through impatience with waiting their turn or from a sense of adventure! They fled their homes, their families and everything that was familiar to them because they had no choice. They, like many others, feared for their lives. These voices are heard directly in the stories of Yassar, Jim and Philip. The strengths of the young people's resistance against the abuse and trauma created by the situations from which they were fleeing and in their journeys from Afghanistan and other countries, is evident in the lengths to which they went to escape these situations and to cope with their incarceration. The notion of queue jumping is meaningless in the context of the lives of these young men. There simply were no queues to jump. The narratives of their travel to Australia and their incarceration refer to experiences that can be described within child welfare discourse as child abuse, both physical and emotional. The abuse, as described by Yassar, commenced in their home countries at the hands of the Taliban and other groups, while their experiences of detention in Australia, present as a continuation of abuse and an exacerbation of previous traumas.

Exacerbation of previous traumas is the theme taken up in the chapter by Fran Gale and Michael Dudley. In their essay they draw on their observations of children and families, as well as testimonies shared with them during visits to the immigration detention centres. Their graphic and personal descriptions of the conditions under which asylum seeking children and their families are detained in Australia, reinforce and extend the details provided in the narratives of Yassar, Jim and

Philip. Gale and Dudley make clear the long term negative mental health implications of the conditions of detention and show how actions by detainees, such as self harm and rioting, can be understood as a response to the dehumanising experiences of detention. In rendering visible a group otherwise generally invisible, they describe how the horrific conditions of life for the children and families in immigration detention centres are maintained by a lack of processes for government accountability.

Jackie Everett, in highlighting the conflict between the values driving current immigration detention policies and the values and attitudes espoused by Australians in previous eras, begins to identify the impact of current policies in defining contemporary Australians. She describes contradictions between contemporary attitudes and strategies of key policymakers and Australia's obligations under international conventions, as well as the contrast between Australia's policies and more generous policies towards asylum seekers of other countries. Furthermore, Everett draws attention to the incongruity in our acknowledging some children, whom we can identify as belonging to us, as vulnerable, while exploiting the vulnerability of 'Others', whom we distance as children of those labeled potentially dangerous. The Australian described by this process does not value or seek to protect all children, this Australian only acts to help those children deemed valuable or 'ours'.

The narratives of the young people and the chapters by Gale and Dudley and by Everett demonstrate the disjuncture between the 'truths' (Gale and Dudley) of detainees' lives, and the politicians' descriptions of their behavior as deviant or evil. They begin to challenge the dominant discourse about who is seeking asylum and why, but more than this they also begin to challenge the legitimacy (ethicalness, morality, appropriateness) of our response. What are we doing to ourselves as a nation by responding so harshly to these people? These chapters foreground questions as to how the hardline approach can be maintained, to what purpose and at what cost? These and other questions are elaborated on and responded to in later chapters.

In her chapter, Mary Crock explores how the contradictions in current immigration detention policies are perpetuated by strategies ostensibly designed to control and deter asylum seeking behavior. She highlights the paradox that Australian policymakers, while asserting lack of jurisdiction for resolving the plight of those rescued from the

Tampa, did nevertheless take responsibility for them, assuming considerable financial costs for Australia in 'off shore' detention of the refugees. In focusing on the legal context for Australia's policies, Crock identifies the ways in which deficits and ambiguities in state and international law around refugees provide the basis for political manipulation. In particular, a lack of formal legal mechanisms has meant that there is no obvious international forum in which Australia can be held to account for its actions towards the asylum seekers.

Chris Sidoti in his chapter also places the Australian Government's policies and practices towards asylum seekers and refugees in the international context. He demonstrates that these policies and practices are gross violations of major international human rights treaties in many ways. The explicit objective specified as the rationale for current policies — deterrence — has been declared as never justifiable by international legal experts, as has arbitrary detention and the lack of provisions for challenging proceedings. Sidoti highlights the ways in which these and other aspects of current policies breach human rights principles and at the same time risk dehumanising those who are citizens of Australia. He enunciates twelve principles on which to base a more just alternative approach to asylum seekers and a model for implementing such an approach. This model recognises the rights of Australia to regulate entry of aliens and provides for the recognition of the human rights of asylum seekers in a way that would financially cost us less than the current system. Such an approach may also cost less in another system of accounting that takes a broader view of what is valuable.

Michael Head turns the whole construction of refugees around, challenging notions of national sovereignty. He situates Australia's actions towards the refugees on board the Tampa in relation to global issues contributing to the contemporary worldwide refugee crisis. He relates the dramatic increase in those fleeing their countries of birth, in the last two decades of the twentieth century, to oppressive economic and political processes and consequent attempts by those suffering from poverty to change their situation, by seeking residence elsewhere. Head argues that within the global context there is a conflict, between the upholding of the principle of national sovereignty, so strongly enunciated by the Howard Government, and the rights of the large numbers of persons seeking asylum. He identifies that the attempts of governments, and in particular the Australian Government, to stem this flow has been facilitated by a narrowness of the Refugee Convention drafted for different times and conditions. The importance of developing an international policy framework towards refugees, based on the concept of global citizenship is identified. This policy would assert a fundamental democratic right to freedom of movement and residence within a global society, to those suffering under intolerable economic and political situations. Such a perspective clearly places Australia as part of a global community.

The chapter by Michael Darcy and Natalie Bolzan returns to the Australian domestic context, highlighting political factors hinted at in earlier chapters, which contributed to and were part of, the Howard Government's construction of an exclusivist identity for Australia. They describe the ways in which the government secured political support for policies to exclude asylum seekers, constructing them as very different from 'us', those already resident in Australia. Darcy and Bolzan include in their analysis of discourses around asylum seekers, discussion of findings from research on the attitudes of young people in New South Wales around asylum seeking issues. The comments of the young people reflected the dominant discourse as portrayed in the media, gave evidence of an alternative discourse and indicated an understanding of the dynamics of the debate, which in some respects paralleled the analysis of this chapter.

The concluding comment of a young person in the Darcy and Bolzan chapter echoed a sentiment that was expressed in other chapters. This was the concern that individually and as a nation, if we are to be comfortable with our own humanity we must take seriously issues of social justice for those who seek asylum by fleeing to Australia.

The last word comes from Chris Sidoti, bringing the discussion up to the current time in terms of how the Government's construction of asylum seekers has and continues to be, challenged by many voices, both locally and internationally. Interestingly the Government's construction is also seen to have gained support internationally, as the Blair Government pursued off shore detention options not dissimilar to the Howard Government's 'Pacific' solution. Sidoti argues there are five issues requiring priority attention, the last of which concerns the hard line and intransigent stance of the Howard Government to the plight of refugees.

In summary, the chapters in this book when taken together provide an understanding and a repudiation of the dominant discourse on asylum seekers, as articulated by politicians. It begins to explore the costs of the dominant discourse and offers alternative ways of responding to the plight of those seeking asylum in Australia. The challenge of the alternative discourse is most tellingly summed up by the juxtaposition of the final comment by a young asylum seeker in an early chapter and the comment of the young Australian in a later chapter. Jim in commenting on his experience of immigration detention policies in Australia states:

> Apart from the (in)humane aspect … you feel really lonely, you feel you are just a number, nobody.

A young Australian provides a reply, significant for us as individuals and as a nation:

> Helping someone makes you feel good at the end of the day … whereas when you don't help them and just avoid them, you're going to have something empty, always, inside.

REFERENCES

Ahwan, L. (2002), 'Children freed from Woomera "barbarism"', *The Daily Telegraph*, 24 Jan 2002, p. 9.

Allard, T. (2001), 'Reith links boat people, terror fight War on America: The Allied Response', *Sydney Morning Herald*, 14 Sept 2001, p. 6.

Allard, T. & Clennell, A. (2001), 'Howard links terrorism to boat people', *Sydney Morning Herald*, 8 Nov 2001, p. 6.

Burke, K. (2001), 'For the sake of the children', *Sydney Morning Herald*, 27 Oct 2001, p. 34.

Cock, A. & Ludlow, M. (2001), 'SINK OR SWIM — Boat people throw children overboard', *The Daily Telegraph*, 8 Oct 2001, p. 1.

Douez, S. & Forbes, M. (2001), 'Boat people "threw children overboard"', *The Age*, 8 Oct 2001, p. 1.

Kevin, T. (2004), *A Certain Maritime Incident: the sinking of SIEV X*. Scribe Publications: Carlton North.

Madigan, M., Dunn, M. & Buttler, D. (2002), 'Protest children removed', *Herald Sun*, 24 Jan 2002, p. 5.

Marr, D. & Wilkinson, M. (2003), *Dark Victory*. Allen & Unwin: Sydney.

Taylor, K. (2002), 'Ruddock removes children', *The Age*, 24 Jan 2002, p. 1.

Weller, P. (2002), *Don't Tell The Prime Minister*. Scribe Publications: Carlton North.

CHAPTER ONE
YASSER

JUDY CASHMORE

This is a story from a young Hazara student who fled Afghanistan at the insistence of his father, to escape the fate of his counterparts who were taken by the Taliban to clear landmines and to act as battlefield shields.

The Hazara people of Afghanistan are a culturally distinct group who have suffered many decades of persecution within Afghanistan. This intensified with the ascendancy of the Taliban, particularly because of their adherence to the Shia sect of Islam.

Yasser tells the story of his life in Afghanistan including his incarceration and beating as a 10 year old during a civil war in his area, his student days and the reason that his father was keen to save him from further strife and persecution. He has also outlined his lonely journey via Pakistan and Indonesia followed by a perilous boat journey to Australia.

Yasser was released from detention fairly quickly on a temporary protection visa and was learning English to help in getting a job when he wrote this memoir.

A Short Memoir of Yasser

I was born in a small village in Afghanistan in 1980. I have four brothers and one sister. My mother died when I was ten years old, but my father is alive. All of my brothers and my sister are older than I am and live in the same village.

When I was five years old, I went to school and learned the holy book — Koran. I studied in primary school for seven years and secondary school for three years. I finished there in 1995.

From that time I can remember two things clearly. One was bad and the other good.

When I was 10 years old, a small war started in our village. The party my brother was supporting was defeated and he had to escape. The opposing party which won took me away to prison. They beat me for ten nights and kept me in jail for one month. I was a very small child and the life in prison was hard and difficult for me. The most painful thing was the death of my mother while I was in jail. This was a bad time and there were many other bad times.

One good memory I have is of being first in my class for those eight years in school. My student days were very enjoyable for me.

In 1996 I went to a town in Northern Afghanistan to further my education. I successfully passed the examination test to allow me to study engineering. I studied there for two years. During those years I witnessed three big wars. In the first war, many people were killed and murdered. My classmate was killed by the Taliban Party. It was a very dangerous time for me and I hid.

This time the Taliban failed so after two days we came out of hiding. Near the University I saw that at least 200 people had been killed. Many of them were old men and women and children. In other places I saw that more than 300 people had been killed. I was shocked, confused and very sad. This was the first war and many buildings, houses, shops and markets had been destroyed.

The second war was also started by the Taliban. Pakistan helped them kill many more poor people. During this time I was in my second semester. Unfortunately the University had to close. These times were very dangerous for me. The Taliban warplanes bombarded all around me and I had to lie down on the earth to save myself.

At the end of 1997, I was attending my fourth semester. Just as the studies were finishing, the Taliban started war again. They succeeded in capturing all of Northern Afghanistan and killed many people in Hazora and Ozback. We escaped to the mountains and then to the desert. Many people rode on a truck which went very fast through the crowd on the road. I was knocked down and I fainted. My feet hurt so much. The truck stopped and I was able to ride in it. My feet hurt for three more months and I limped about my room. All the time I was jobless.

After about four months, the Taliban came to our village and harassed our people. They took money from us and things from our shops without paying for them. They used force against us all the time and tried to make us change our religion. This made us very sad. For seven months they beat us and bullied us. Many people were arrested and made to collect land mines. Many were killed doing this and others had their hands and feet blown off.

Because the Taliban terrorised our people more and more, we lost our patience and, even though we did not have any guns, we drove the Taliban out of our village. For one year, our village was free of the Taliban but then they sent a representative to our leader. He said that if we did not let them return, they would invade and destroy us. We could not prevent them from coming back. They terrorised us again and stopped all mail to us, closed our schools and prevented us from leaving our village. It was like a prison.

In July 2000, a Taliban representative came to our village. They took many young men to clear landmines and to act as battlefield shields. When I heard about this, I feared that I would be captured and I escaped to the mountains. I stayed in hiding for about four days. My father came and took me to a market place in Jaooz Barga and introduced me to a person who knew a smuggler in Gazni. This person took me to introduce me to a smuggler who agreed to take me to Pakistan and then to Australia.

From Afghanistan, I traveled to Pakistan with the smuggler. We came through mountain passes to Pakistan because the Taliban Party did not want us to get out of the county alive. I was in Pakistan for twenty days. During these twenty days, I was hidden by the smuggler, because we were illegal immigrants. I then flew to Indonesia using a false passport. I stayed in Indonesia for five days, then I boarded a boat to Australia. In Indonesia we were treated very badly by the smuggler. We were hidden and we had only a little food at lunch and at night time. It was a very bad time, especially for me because I got malaria fever in Indonesia. I was alone, sick, unhappy, without hope, food, money or family, nothing. We were afraid of the Indonesian Police because they searched everywhere to find illegal passengers and took many of them to jail.

We stayed for five days in Indonesia — a dangerous five days. The smuggler took a boat and sent us to Australia. We were at sea for 10 days. Our boat was very small, with 101 people onboard. There were six families and the rest were single men. We were very crowded. We did not have enough spaces for sleeping or sitting. Our conditions weren't good. For the first two days, the sea was very stormy, the boat was shaking and moving. We all got motion sickness and we were vomiting everything we ate. There was not enough food or water to drink but we were sick to eat anything. The condition of the women and children was very bad, they had no place to sleep, so they were very tired. During the ten days we sailed night and day without sighting land. On the ninth night our boat become holed and the waters were coming inside our boat. We were confused and feared for our lives. We all used dishes to bail out the boat, but not as fast as the water came in. We did it for five hours. We got tired, hungry and thirsty, but suddenly saw an Australian patrol boat. They came and rescued our lives. They gave us two water pumps for getting out the water. Unfortunately they said they would repair our boat and we would be sent back to Indonesia.

The patrol boat brought us to Darwin, Australia. We had two interviews in camp and then they sent me to ... Next we flew to Curtin camp in Derby, Western Australia. I stayed in the camp for one month and now I am waiting here in ...

The future for Yasser is uncertain as when his temporary protection visa expires he may be forcibly repatriated to Afghanistan.

CHAPTER TWO
'JUST NOBODIES'

THE DOUBLE JEOPARDY OF REFUGEE CHILDREN 'JIM' AND 'PHILIP'

JAN MASON

It has been noted by Dennis McNamara, former director, Division of International Protection United Nations High Commissioner for Refugees that refugee children suffer double jeopardy, firstly as a consequence of the denial of human rights that have resulted in their refugee status; secondly as refugee children they are particularly vulnerable to abuse. Refugee children who are not with adult family members when they seek asylum are particularly vulnerable to abuse or 'retraumatisation' (McNamara, 1999).

Until recently the voices of adult refugees have rarely been heard in public forums in Australia. It is hardly surprising in a country where children generally are seldom audible in the media and other public forums, that little has been heard of the voices of child refugees. In these circumstances the actions of refugee children in sewing their lips and the media reporting of it (Sydney Morning Herald, 2002; Taylor, 2002), conveyed with powerful irony the significance of policies around asylum seekers which continue to render these children as mute.

Therefore when two young boys seeking refugee status requested of one of us to help them to be heard, we considered it important that we give their voices a key role in the seminar on Children and Families in Refugee Detention Centres (4th March 2002, University of Western Sydney) and in this book.

In the process of the presentation of the boys' stories at the seminar, the irony of the sewn lips of young refugees was perpetuated by the lengths to which we deemed it necessary to go to to preserve their anonymity for fear of provoking recriminations to the boys as a result of their sharing with us their experiences. I have made editorial amendments to the stories only to clarify the points they made through an interpreter and to de identify them. We have given the two boys English names to avoid any risks of mistaken identity for other Afghan young people. Questions from the interviewer have been omitted to present the boys' stories in more narrative form.

Why and How the Boys came to Australia

In their interview Jim and Philip told the interviewer that they came to Australia because their lives were in danger if they stayed in Afghanistan. Philip explained that his father had been taken by the Taliban:

> ... and still I do not know where is my father. My brother was killed by the Taliban and that's why my mother decided that I should come to Australia or some where else.

Both boys continued to be confronted by danger on their voyage to Australia.

Jim describes how after his overland trek and voyage to Indonesia he finally found a boat to bring him to Australia:

> And then we came to Australia by boat. We did not believe we would be alive when we arrive to Australia because when we see the boat it was very dangerous ... we didn't believe we would get to Australia ... the ocean is very dangerous and the boat felt like this (places hands together and swings vigorously from side to side) ... there was about one hundred and three people on the boat, you sit like this (hunches up) because you are very close —
>
> For 13 days we didn't sleep and not enough food, just little ... some eggs or just like rice — there is nothing else. For 13 days I ate just three or four eggs but nothing else.

Both boys describe how after arriving at different times in Australian waters off Derby, they were processed by officials. During this time Jim was on Christmas Island and Philip remained on the boat, each for over a week.

Life in a Detention Centre

Jim and Philip were then detained in the same detention centre. Jim describes his early experience of this place:

> I didn't know anyone. There is like two part. In one 'camp' ... one of them is like free, the people go ... This section where you can

move around … they call it like a 'free' camp … and the next is very closed, you can't go outside.

I was in the section where I couldn't move out for 25 days then after 25 days they let me go to the other section. When I finished the second interview then I moved to the other camp with more freedom.

Jim describes the section where he was unable to more around:

That is not a good place … very closed. No place to play, and it's very bad situation for 25 days.

Philip described his main memories of the detention centre as being:

Lot's of pressure. The first time — after two months the case officer refuse me, refused my application. After two months I went to the tribunal and they take a long time — two months. They make appointment for me, it takes a long time, two months.

Then I went again. Again two months and I was accepted by the tribunal. Another two months they give me the visa, then I came out from detention. The waiting was very hard for us. Difficult. Everyone, my friends there they released and I (stayed there) by myself.

In describing his experiences of the detention centre, Jim said:

We are like in one room, like 20 beds, is like for under eighteen (years old). So we all like brothers live in one room, like very close friends. So when one of them like me and anyone else come out … everyone they cry because it's a bad situation … especially it is very hot. So we're walking about in the room So we can't go outside because it's very, very hot. The police didn't let us to go outside … all close to you, not very far like this (hunches up showing how cramped the room was) you can't move … It's all so hot and there's no tree so we can't go outside. That's why we stay in my room and talking together. So when someone come out they get their visa and everyone cry for two/three days … Because they do not have any friend.

Jim described how in the centre:

we can't play, like there is special time in the afternoon (for play). Like two/three hours … Like especially the food, you can't get every kind of food that you want, so we can't get it, we didn't have a good choice … you can't talk to different people, just stay in your room and don't speak. If you're like me and three people in one room you can speak with these people but not with other people from other countries. If you ask why you're told 'shut up, no why (questions?).

The translator clarified that there were people of different nationalities in the room but the boys were only allowed to talk with those of the same nationality.

Philip said that he had problems with the daily routine and the problems he had with the time he spent in detention:

> ... very hard, it was long time there. Nine months there ... very hard spending my time, because it is boring, no possibility for us. There was not very much to do. Just breakfast time, lunch time, dinner time and there was one hours/two hours we could just play the soccer. That's it.

Jim:

> I knew people in my room, that's all and at six o'clock we come out. And specially there is no good education in the detention centre. Just like at five o'clock or four o'clock there is just some time, not all the time ... if you want the teacher gives you a paper if you want (so that you are) learning some words, that's all ... Maybe three days a week for just one hour.

Insecurity About the Visa Application Decision Making Process

Philip discussed his experiences as related to a lack of information about the decision making process:

> Where we were in the camp sometimes the authority played like a kind of mind game with us. Like I had my visa, they told me I had been accepted, can have the visa, but they didn't give it to me for two and a halfmonth. They didn't release me from the camp. And that happened to many other people in our room, in our area. That caused lots of riots and anger and that was one of the reasons people they wanted, you know, to go for the hunger strike and things like that because sometimes people they knew, they have gone through all the process, the process has been finished, they have answered, but they don't give them the answer or they don't let them go.

> ... sometimes after they did interviews with people about twenty, twenty five people at the one day, and some of them they release in twelve days, ten days but they kept the rest for two months, three months, four months. We did not understand the reason for that and that caused lots of tension with us because we knew we had been accepted, we knew basic rights. We knew we had to go to interview we had to get the visa to be able to go out, things like that. But the timing we did not really understand, why some people go to ten days

but the rest of us we didn't. We asked for lawyer, some legal aid but they didn't really pay attention, they didn't say no or yes. They just said we didn't have time today or we do this in the future or next week. And that delay time caused lots of tension with people.

Jim said:

> ... [there] is no discussion, no talk about what condition or which state of processing you are in. Its just like interview, you go to your room and ... the person you are dealing with is your case officer and the case officer and the case officer ... you don't see them until they need you again. That's it.

The translator clarified that Jim said they were told they could not have access to a lawyer; they were not given this option. The only person who deals with the detainees was the case officer and the detainees could only talk to this person when they were called for, the detainees could not initiate discussion or ask them questions.

Jim added:

> it is a one sided thing and you are not even allowed to ask question

and described the feelings associated with these experiences of uncertainty.

> Everyone is feeling ... like most people crying, as well because some of the people they cannot very easily go out, especially the under eighteen's ... they do nothing ... They didn't exactly answer you. Like — you have this wrong answer or you have answer (after) maybe three or four question so that is why we can't accept you now. It takes like one or two months ...

In answer to questions of an official:

> He said no, you should just wait, it is not your business you should just stay in your room. That's all.

> ... so (for) most of people (it has) some effect in their mind ... and the new thing like 15 or 20 people did not eat for three days. And the police didn't come and ask why you don't eat. Why you don't eat food, what is the reason? ...

> Just they come, tell the number; it is your number — yes, that is all. And some people they like, put the knife here (gesturing to arm and leg) ... because they become very worried or unhappy about detention centre ... with a knife or something else cutting.

> [Because this] has a big effect on your mind ... the people did not like to stay there. (It was) a bad situation. Like most of the people in very, very bad situation in Afghanistan, they come here and some

peoples cutting here ... they don't like to stay more because of problem about talking to case officer ... but no answer and they can't go outside. And the police didn't say about what happened with you so that's why'.

Philip told the interviewer about his incident of self-harm:

One of the people that hurt themselves was me. Because I had an operation in Afghanistan on my ankle and my ankle was hurting a lot ... for a few weeks. One night I was asking them to do something to let me go or do exercise ... I need to see a doctor. And they said you are not here permanently, you are temporary — we can't do anything, you have to wait. And after I have my visa they do not let me go for two and a half months and I just kept going to them and asking and asking all the time ... my ankle was hurting so much, I was not sleeping much and I was really distressed and really, really in anger and I took a razor and I was cutting myself.

Nobody came to see what was happening. I went to the medical room, I went to the nurse and nurse says, what's happening and I said my ankle is hurting and I showed my ankle with the blood there and she calls the police and police came and took me to the small room, we called that room X. It's just a dark room, very small dark room and they kept me there for about five days. Then after five days I was crying and I tell them I don't hurt myself please let me go. It was just me ... there were six or seven Iranian guys and the same thing happened they were taken to separate rooms.

The Isolation Room

There was a camera in the corner. The room was:

... smaller than this room (about 3 x 4 metres). Camera there, there is no chair to sit down. This if for punishment, there is just a small hole for bit of light coming and all around is the camera.

They kept me in the room because:

they wanted me to say why I did hurt myself. They just kept asking why I hurt myself. I said I was in pain, I went to the medical ... and ask for tablets for pain killer and sleeping and they just kept ignoring me.

She just cleaned the blood and put on a patch of gauze, that's it. When you are in the X room if you eat and you behave they let you go. If you don't they just keep you there for longer. There were people there longer time than five days, six days ...

This was kind of like a mental game for me. I saw an Iranian guy — he was there about twenty days refusing to eat and they used to — police used to come and force him to eat and give him some kind of food injection for not eating.

Jim:

The people they didn't like to eat … If I die it is better than … this place … For 15–20 days some people didn't eat something. The people fainted they become like … unconscious … that's why the people didn't eat something … His legs (referring to Philip) operation from here to here is very pain(ful), he can't sleep and he tell like twenty time the doctor, the nurse. (He) said I have this pain, I can't sleep, I can't walk and she said wait, wait there is no chance for you now at the moment. So he began to cut here so … and he go to doctor but the police send (him) to (isolation area) bad place and then … nothing else.

The Camp and Mental Instability

Phillip describes how people react in the camp to the conditions:

The whole condition in the camp is really, really bad people are really stressed. Those people they are there for a long time they get really agitated. They used to come to restaurant for example … a guy sits there for a while and then he gets really upset, mentally sick and he just pulls the chair and throws it away and causes lots of fight and scaredness between people — young people children — because the restaurant if for everybody, everybody is there … And each time people they go to restaurant for lunch, dinner they are always cautious and careful because something might come up …

Jim adds:

The next thing is like people go on the tree, they climb on the tree very high … they say I want to kill myself, I don't like to stay here and the police one time say, don't do that and that's all. And the second time the police say … if you want to, kill yourself … they didn't care about it. The police say if you want to kill yourself you can.

Education

Philip said:

There is no good education inside of the camp … where people going to get education … like English language centre … I would have liked (to learn) English ... there is not possible class to go to get education.

Jim explained he wanted to learn the English language but:

what we had which was like for just one hour the people go like everyone go to class one day the teacher is absent — not coming ... I wanted to study English, like grammar that we can get English, speak English like school like children for young people so everybody wanted to study. Everyone had a problem they did not have a serious class, only one day someone talking about Australia.

Changes that could Improve the Situation of Young Asylum Seekers in Australia

In response to this question Jim stated:

If they want to make detention Centres ... I think there should be good education in the detention centre ... and the next thing is exercise and the third ... is the people should go like small picnic outside. Just ... it should be like go outside walking or swimming or something else ...

The police should ask that what is your problem— why you are not eating the food and if you sickyou should go see the doctor. The police like they come just talk very seriously, what is your number, they had like a card when you go to food and they say are you here, you say yes, give me your number. You show the number that's all.

Philip agreed with Jim that education would help with life in a detention centre:

but also for application process to be a bit quicker. Especially for young people its very demoralising being there for long time because there is nothing there to do and they got lots of energy and sometimes we get really, really frustrated there.

Those people of more mature age they have more understanding of time but younger people they don't, they don't know what to do with their time and it is frustrating.

In response to the interviewer's question about whether names are used by officials in the detention centres, Jim stated:

No, no just number. Like my number was 0001. They call me 0001 that's all. Not name.

Philip added:

Yes they call you number. 0009 my number (laughs a little).

Jim's experience of being called by a number was that:

apart from the(in)humane aspect of it you feel really lonely when they call you with number because you are used to your name, people communicate with you with your name, when they call you with the number you feel really lonely, you feel you are just a number, nobody.

REFERENCES

McNamara, D. (1999), 'Refugee children', in Human Rights Watch (Ed.), *Promises Broken: An Assessment of Children's Rights on the 10th Anniversary of the Convention on the Rights of the Child.*
http://hrw.org/campaigns/crp/promises/refugees.html
Sydney Morning Herald (2002), 'Lip sewing', 21 Jan 2002, p. 10.
Taylor, K. (2002), 'Ruddock removes children', *The Age*, 24 Jan 2002, p. 1.

CHAPTER THREE

DURABLE SOLUTIONS OR POLITICS OF MISERY?

REFUGEE PROTECTION IN AUSTRALIA AFTER *TAMPA*

MARY CROCK

Points of Embarcation

In his article examining the implications of the 'Tampa Affair' from the perspective of international maritime law, Associate Professor Don Rothwell provides the following summary of the events that represent the starting point for a symposium and workshop on the now notorious ' Tampa Affair':

> On 26 August 2001, the Australian Search and Rescue organisation (AusSAR) assisted in the coordination of a search and rescue operation in the Indian Ocean for the Palapa 1, an Indonesian flagged ship carrying 433 people. The Norwegian flagged roll on/roll off container ship, MV Tampa, responded to this request and with the assistance of the Australian authorities was guided to the sinking vessel where it successfully carried out the rescue operation. Immediately following the rescue, the Tampa headed towards the Indonesian port of Merak, some 246 nautical miles to the north. However, approximately four hours into this voyage, the Tampa reversed course and began steaming south towards the Australian territory of Christmas Island, which had only been 75 nautical miles south of where the original rescue had taken place. Later that evening the master of the Tampa, Captain Rinnan, was asked by Australian authorities to change course for Indonesia and threatened that if he did enter Australia's territorial sea with the intention of offloading the persons rescued from the Palapa 1 that he would be subject to prosecution under the Migration Act 1958 (Cth) for people smuggling. This communication gave the first clear indication of the position the Australian government was taking towards the Tampa and set the tone for the Australian government's legal and policy response over the course of the next week (Rothwell, 2002:118).[1]

The sequelae to Captain Rinnan's gesture in rescuing the 433 aboard the KM Palapa 1 and making for Australia's Christmas Island are the stuff of history. Not only did the Australian Government refuse the Tampa the right to offload its human cargo on Australian soil, but the incident became the basis for blocking the admission of all further boat people; for the 'excision' from Australia's 'migration zone' of external territories such as Christmas Island; and for the establishment of an elaborate and expensive program for the deflection of asylum seekers to the Pacific Islands of Nauru, Papua New Guinea and New Zealand.

In this article, I will examine what I identify as three phases of the Tampa Affair and its aftermath, setting out the main legal issues that arose and situating the actions taken within the context of law and contemporary politics. The first phase relates to the events surrounding and following the rescue of the 433 individuals plucked from the sinking MV Palapa 1. The second concerns to the establishment of the so called 'Pacific Solution', including the creation of detention facilities on Nauru and PNG's Manus Island. The third involves the more recent passage of legislation allowing for the transportation to Australia of individuals detained offshore, drawing in a discussion of changes to onshore processing and entitlements affecting refugees in Australia.

My basic thesis will be that international law — in particular international refugee law — provides surprisingly little in the way of a rights regime for asylum seekers who take to the seas in their quest for safe haven. Even if it can be argued that Australia has been in breach of its obligations under the Convention relating to the Status of Refugees, relevant state practice is ambiguous and there is no obvious forum in which Australia can be held to account for any breach.

The problem is that within the various legal frameworks relevant to the Tampa Affair, plausible arguments can be made both for and against the actions taken by the Australian Government. The ambiguity of the law makes the incident and its aftermath a fertile field for jurisprudential and sociological debate. At the same time, the Tampa Affair also represents a fascinating case study of how formalistic characterisations of the Rule of Law can be manipulated for political ends. It will be my argument that Australia's adherence to the Rule of Law in recent times has become increasingly formalistic: to the point that we appear at times to come close to paying lip service to obligations assumed as a matter of international law.

In the wake of the attacks in America on 11 September 2002, the Howard Coalition Government's tough line on asylum seekers helped to win a federal election. The Government used the threat represented by unauthorised arrivals to strike fear into the heart of the Australian electorate, fanning concerns by allowing the dissemination of false accounts of asylum seekers throwing children into the ocean. The culture of self-harm that has come to permeate the immigration detention facilities has been used as further evidence of 'alien', un-Australian behaviour. Its tactics threw the Opposition Labor Party into disarray. In the words of John Button (2002):

> The most profoundly disillusioning event in 2001 for those who believed in a humanitarian and compassionate Labor Party was its response to the Tampa incident and the engineered refugee crisis. People searched in vain for a sign of difference between the ALP and the Coalition. On 19 October it became clear there was none. On that day some 350 asylum seekers were drowned when an overcrowded Indonesian fishing vessel sank off the coast of Java. The husband of one survivor, a woman whose three young children had drowned, was living in Australia on a temporary protection visa. The Immigration Minister, Philip Ruddock, refused to waive the conditions of the visa, effectively preventing the husband from visiting his wife in Indonesia. This was an inhumane and cruel decision, and Kim Beazley acquiesced in it (2002,16).

The Labor leadership had overlooked the fact that the potentially explosive issue of 'boat people' had been on the public agenda since early in 2001. As a result they were left stunned and flatfooted. No alternative was suggested. It did not seem to matter that the platform of the party, updated at the National Conference in August 2000, contained a clear and compassionate statement of principle in relation to asylum seekers and refugees (ALP, 2000).

The ALP was caught in the headlights, frozen between the sentiment of the national platform and belief in compassionate, humane values on the one hand and opinion polls on the other. Labor's confusion was ruthlessly exploited by Howard and his henchmen Reith, Costello and Ruddock. Howard played two cards, one of which seemed suspiciously like racism, the other involving a spurious appeal to a busstop egalitarianism. This second card said: these people are not victims but selfish 'queue jumpers' unprepared to wait for entry to the promised land. Australians, sometimes uncertain about their own motives, were provided with an alibi: I'm not a racist, just a fervent believer in queues.

Button could have added that Prime Minister Howard's political play at home was replicated at an international level. The Australian Government backed the United Nation's High Commission for Refugees (UNHCR) into an uncomfortable corner, with it, the International Organisation for Migration (IOM). The two agencies agreed to take responsibility for processing the refugee claims of the asylum seekers from the Tampa and from the Acheng, a second vessel intercepted while en route from Christmas Island. Lucrative deals were brokered with Nauru and New Zealand then with Papua New Guinea to set up detention facilities that place both Nauru and the PNG Government's in breach of their domestic human rights laws (Ruddock, 2002).

Australia's behaviour has done little to enhance its international reputation as a humanitarian nation. Allegations of breaches of its 'strict' international legal obligations may be difficult to substantiate.

However, from a broader legal perspective — most notably from the perspective of international human rights law and what is sometimes referred to as 'soft' international law — Australia's policies and behaviour are less defensible. There may not be obvious mechanisms for bringing Australia to account: the close alliance between Australia and the United States gives the country a powerful protector. However, in the longer term, it is not likely that history will look kindly on this phase of Australia's history.

Phase 1 of the *Tampa* Affair: The Perils of Sea Rescues in the Age of Terror

The *Tampa* Incident

The standoff that developed between Captain Rinnan of the Tampa and the Australian Government in late August 2001 raised questions of law in at least three broad areas: international maritime law, international refugee law and domestic migration law.[1] Overlaying these legal contexts, the situation becomes further complicated when sited within the historical events of September 2001. It is well to recall that the decision of the Federal Court in the litigation induced by the *Tampa* standoff (Victorian Council for Civil Liberties and Ors v Minister, 2001; Vadarlis v Ruddock, 2001)[1] was handed down only hours before the terrorist attacks in America on September 11. The horrific events of that day hang over the *Tampa* Affair. They help to explain why public opinion in Australia firmed so quickly and completely against the boat

26

people and why Prime Minister Howard's use of the fear factor was such a potent weapon.

Legal issues arose under international maritime law for the simple reason that this is the framework that governed Captain Rinnan's immediate behaviour when he encountered the sinking Palapa I. As Rothwell and others have pointed out (2002; Tauman, 2002; Fonteyne, 2001), Captain Rinnan's response in taking all 433 rescuees' on board the *Tampa* exceeded his international legal obligations under international Law of the Sea: the *Tampa* was licenced to carry 50 people and equipped to cater for fewer still. Christmas Island being the closest landfall from the point of rescue, there are also strong grounds for arguing that the law of the sea entitled him to unload the rescued persons on that piece of Australian territory (O'Connell, 1984:85557). Conversely, Australia's behaviour in boarding the *Tampa* and taking control of the vessel under armed guard, together with its closure of Flying Fish Cove are difficult to justify. Although the Norwegian captain was threatened with fines as a people smuggler, he clearly did not fit this description. Given the state of the rescuees and the captain's belief that he would have deaths on board if medical assistance was not obtained as a matter of urgency, there are strong grounds for arguing that the legal principles of necessity and force majeure justified his insistence on pursuing landfall on Christmas Island (Rothwell, 2002:12324).

Australia's answer to these allegations was to assert that the usual practice in situations of maritime emergencies is for the vessel taking on rescued persons to continue on its planned route as nearly as possible, disembarking rescuees at a convenient port. In this instance, Merak in Indonesia was said to have fitted the bill. This port is situated in the same general direction as the *Tampa* 's original planned route to Singapore and has a harbour rated to take a vessel the size of the *Tampa*. Australia's actions at each stage were defended as being consistent with its status as a sovereign nation whose national security is dependant on control of its borders.

The picture becomes more complex when the viewer's frame of reference is altered so as to view the events through the additional portal of international refugee law. It was apparent from very early in the piece that the *Tampa* rescuees wished to seek asylum in Australia on the basis that they were refugees (Hathaway, 2001:39). Throughout the initial crisis period their status as refugees had not been determined. At best they could be characterised as 'asylum seekers'. The basic problem facing refugee claimants is that the Refugee Convention does not provide a right to claim asylum. This point has been made forcefully by Gummow J:

> First, it has long been recognised that, according to customary international law, the right of asylum is a right of States, not of the individual; no individual, including those seeking asylum, may assert a right to enter the territory of a State of which that individual is not a national ... The proposition that every State has competence to regulate the admission of aliens at will was applied in Australian municipal law from the earliest days of this Court ... However, from that proposition, two principles of customary international law have followed. One is that a State is free to admit anyone it chooses to admit, even at the risk of inviting the displeasure of another State; and the other is that, because no State is entitled to exercise corporeal control over its nationals on the territory of another State, such individuals are safe from further persecution unless the asylum State is prepared to surrender them ... A corollary is that, in the absence of an extradition treaty, the asylum State has no international obligation to surrender fugitives to the State from which they have fled ... and the fugitives are protected against the exercise of jurisdiction by that State (Minister for Immigration and Multicultural Affairs v Ibrahim, 2000:para 137).

Having said this, even if the *Tampa* rescuees could invoke no right to seek asylum in Australia, the fact that their refugee status had not been determined at the time of their interception at sea did not mean that the Refugee Convention offered them no succour. Under this Convention, the status of refugee is not 'created' by any determination process. People either are, or are not, refugees depending on the applicability of the definition of refugee at a particular point in time. Put another way, the obligations imposed by the Refugee Convention are not dependant on refugees having their status recognised. On this view, the burning issue in the *Tampa* standoff was not so much the status of each of the rescuees or their right to claim asylum. It was the extent and nature of Australia's obligations, assuming that the group included refugees (as defined in the Convention) (Hathaway, 2001:41). Given the fact that the *Tampa* rescuees were mainly from Afghanistan, where the feared Taliban were still in power, such an assumption could hardly be described as farfetched. This point was made by North J in the first instance ruling in the *Tampa* litigation. His Honour said:

It is notorious that a significant proportion of asylum seekers from Afghanistan processed through asylum status systems qualify as refugees under the Convention relating to the Status of Refugees (1951) (the Refugees Convention). Once assessed as refugees, this means that they are recognised as persons fleeing from persecution in Afghanistan. While such people no doubt make decisions about their lives, those decisions should be seen against the background of the pressures generated by flight from persecution (Victorian Council for Civil Liberties and Ors v Minister for Immigration, Multiculturalism and Indigenous Affairs, 2001:471 [para 67]).

Arguments have raged over which country had primary responsibility for the *Tampa* asylum seekers, qua refugees. Australia asserts that Indonesia, as country of embarcation, should have agreed to take them back. Although Indonesia is not a signatory to the Refugee Convention, the argument runs, the predominantly Muslim identity of the rescuees meant that in practical terms they would not face persecution in that country. As a matter of fact, Indonesia had been offering (and continues to offer) de facto protection to asylum seekers from Afghanistan and the Middle East. The problem faced by Australia is that the *Tampa* and Acheng rescuees had not been lawfully present in Indonesia, and there was no basis in international law, or any other law, indicating an obligation of any kind to readmit individuals who had left its shores in such circumstances.

In his commentary on the *Tampa* affair, Hathaway suggests that the two states with primary responsibility for the rescuees were Norway and Australia. Hathaway asserts that in the case of sea rescues, the flag state of a rescue vessel assumes responsibility to ensure that refugees are not refouled to a place where they will face persecution on one of the five Convention grounds (Hathaway, 2001:41, note 11). The problem with this argument is that the *Tampa* was a commercial vessel, albeit registered in Norway, and not sailing under a flag of convenience. The situation might have been more clearcut if the *Tampa* could be characterised as a state vessel to which the full range of state responsibilities under international law would apply (Churchill & Lowe, 1999:257263). Moreover, as many acknowledge (GoodwinGill, 1996:158; Schaeffer, 197880; Pugash, 1977; Tauman, 2002), state practice has varied greatly at the height of refugee crises involving fugitives taking to boats in any numbers.' If any precedents exist for flagship states taking responsibility for refugees rescued at sea, the countries involved have generally been geographically proximate to the scene of the rescue, and have been willing to participate in a management program (Schaeffer, 197880; Pugash, 1977).

Arguments in favour of Australia having primary responsibility for the rescuees have stressed the proximity of Christmas Island to the rescue site; the involvement of the Australian authorities in the initial search and rescue operation; and, ultimately, the presence of the *Tampa* within Australian coastal waters. As a signatory to the Refugee Convention, it is arguable that Australia's primary responsibility was not to refoule or return an assumed refugee to a place of persecution. Hathaway argues with some force that state parties to this Convention cannot as a matter of law avoid their obligations by adopting 'mechanistic' strategies to avoid the assumption of responsibility (2001:41).' The Professor groups together in this respect both the physical expulsion of the *Tampa* and its human cargo and the legislative measures taken to nominally remove Australian jurisdiction.

Cutting across these debates about jurisdiction, what is perhaps most striking throughout the whole *Tampa* Affair is the nature of Australia's actions in resolving the impasse that developed. Although going to great lengths to assert lack of jurisdiction, Australia did — in fact — take responsibility for the rescuees. Whatever the criticisms that can be made of Australia in these early stages of the ' *Tampa* Affair', it could not be said that Australia engaged in 'refoulment' in the sense of sending people back to places where they would face persecution. On the contrary, the involvement of the UNHCR and the IOM ensured that all persons claiming to be refugees would have their refugee claims assessed.

Australia also both bankrolled the major actors (Nauru, Papua New Guinea and the UN agencies) and assumed some responsibility itself for determining the refugee claims of the rescuees. Australia still maintains the tightest control of the centres established in Nauru and in Papua New Guinea, even down to exercising a veto over applications for visas for outsiders to visit those places. If this does not constitute de facto assumption of jurisdiction, it is difficult to see how else to characterise Australia's behaviour.[10]

Operation Relex

The '*Tampa* Affair' was the impetus for a rash of legislative amendments to the Migration Act 1958 (Cth). Although the Labor Opposition opposed the first Border Protection Bill (Hancock, 20012a:3, notes 55 & 56, 20012b), it ultimately combined with the Government to pass no less than seven bills.[11] The Border Protection (Validation and Enforcement Powers) Act 2001 retrospectively validated any action taken by the Commonwealth in relation to the *Tampa,* the Acheng and other ships stopped between 27 August and the date of Royal Assent to the Act. By preventing the commencement or continuance of any civil or criminal proceedings challenging actions covered by the legislation, this legislation helped to stifle appeals from the Federal Court. The Act also conferred extraordinary powers on 'officers' to search, detain and move persons aboard ships that have been pursued, boarded and detained by Australian authorities. Unlike the earlier Bill, there is no requirement that officers boarding a ship act in 'good faith'. The legislation is not limited to actions taken within Australia's territorial sea, nor is any deference made to the constraints on extraterritorial operations imposed by the 1982 UN Convention on the Law of the Sea (UNCLOS) (O'Connell, 1984).

Some commentators assert that the new laws are in breach of Australia's international legal obligations because they authorise Australian 'officers' to operate outside of Australia's territorial jurisdiction (Hancock, 20012a, 20012b; Shearer, 1997:162 164). The legislation certainly goes beyond what has been proposed by the United Nations to combat people smuggling. The Draft Protocol against the Smuggling of Migrants by Land, Air and Sea (supplementing the Draft Convention against Transnational Organised Crime) encourages states to exercise their jurisdiction fully to combat people smuggling (UN, 1999). However, the draft Protocol does not advise states to exceed their jurisdiction. Nor are there any moves to expand the maritime jurisdiction of states under international law.

There were other legislative changes made to underpin 'Operation Relex'. To prevent the use of Christmas Island and of the nearby reefs as delivery points for asylum seekers, the Parliament empowered the Minister to declare parts of Australia's territory to be outside the 'migration zone'. Under the Migration Amendment (Excision from Migration Zone) Act 2001, people coming ashore at Ashmore Reef, on the Keeling or Cocos Islands or on Christmas Island are now deemed not to have entered Australia's migration zone. The legislation introduces the concepts of 'excised offshore places' and 'offshore entry persons' and operates to prevent people on these territories from having the right to access Australia's refugee protection regime.

If Australia can claim (with some justification) that it has not engaged in any practice of refouling the *Tampa* (and Acheng) refugees, the same cannot be said of all of its actions under what is known as 'Operation Relex'. Not much is known of the practical application of the laws and policy adopted following the *Tampa* incident. However, accounts have emerged of Australia interdicting vessels carrying asylum seekers outside of its territorial waters as well as in the immediate proximity of its newly 'excised' territories, and of those vessels being towed or escorted back to Indonesia and West Timor. The intercepted vessels — referred to as 'Suspected Illegal Entry Vessels' or SIEVs — included the now infamous SIEV 4, photographs of which were misused by the Government to promote the fiction of asylum seekers throwing their children overboard to 'blackmail' Australia into accepting them. With a Senate inquiry into this affair and through the work of investigative journalists (for example, Four Corners, 2002) evidence has emerged of Australian involvement in incidents at sea resulting in two confirmed deaths by drowning, and three other suspected drownings. Overshadowing these incidents was the sinking in October 2001 of SIEV X, a boat crammed with mainly Afghan and Iraqi asylum seekers embarking from Indonesia. Over 350 lives were lost. Allegations have emerged of Indonesian officials forcing asylum seekers onto the doomed and overloaded vessel at gunpoint; of the Australian surveillance operations being aware that the vessel had left, but doing nothing to track its passage or to come to the assistance of the asylum seekers in a timely fashion.

The Government strongly resists suggestions that Australia is in any way accountable for these events, arguing that such tragic occurrences simply underscore the hazards of using the offices of people smugglers to try and circumvent regular immigration procedures. While defences may be found to each dreadful incident, the plain truth is that without Australia's harsh policies and attitudes, the probabilities are that these lives would not have been lost.

Although the Government clearly disputes this view, I believe that an argument can be made that Operation Relex does breach the non-refoulement principle. Indonesia is not a signatory to the Refugee Convention. There are a number of asylum seekers living in Indonesia in circumstances that appear to be tolerated by the Indonesian government. However, the SIEV X incident provides a basis for doubting whether the protection offered to Muslim asylum seekers in that country is 'effective' in the sense of providing some form of tenure or sanctuary. The obligation not to refoule refugees to a place where they face persecution extends to indirect as well as direct return (Goodwin Gill, 1996:333344).

Hathaway has argued with conviction that Australia's deflection of the *Tampa* asylum seekers and of subsequent boat people intercepted in what became known as 'Operation Relex' constituted behaviour that penalises the asylum seekers involved because of the alleged illegal mode of their entry. Article 31(1) of the Refugee Convention prohibits state parties from imposing penalties, on account of their illegal entry or presence, on refugees in certain circumstances.

Australia's treatment of both the Pacific Solution asylum seekers and those processed onshore is arguably punitive in nature. Whether Australia is technically in breach of Art 31, however, is a moot point. On its face, Art 31(1) applies to frontline refugee receiving states. The refugees to whom the no penalty provisions apply are those 'coming directly from a territory where their life or freedom was threatened in the sense of Article 1'. The Australian Government's argument is that the boat people intercepted en route to Australia do not meet this description. Indeed, the official Australian line is that the arrivals represent 'secondary refugee flows'. According to Minister Ruddock, the primary goal of the Government in taking its tough stance against asylum seekers is to prevent refugees from 'forum shopping'. The asylum seekers, it is argued, are individuals who have secured safety from persecution in a third country, but who come on to Australia using the services of people smugglers so as to achieve an 'immigration outcome'. The Minister's view is that UN processes are undermined if refugees are allowed to take matters into their own hands, jumping the 'queue' of persons recognised by the UN as refugees and ear marked for resettlement in third countries.[12]

Once again, the overwhelming impression conveyed by this 'official' version is one of formalism and mechanistic opportunism. Accepting this characterisation of fugitives from Afghanistan requires a closedeye approach to the real situation that pertains in the countries through which literally millions of refugees have passed. It also flies in the face of the interpretation of Art 31(1) that UNHCR would like to see countries adopt (GoodwinGill, 2001).

Apart from its formalistic characterisation of its obligations under international refugee law, the second factor operating in the

Government's favour in its brokered resolution of the *Tampa* standoff is the recent American precedent of the US Haitian Interdiction program. That program involved the interception, deflection and sometimes even the direct refoulement of many thousands of boat people emanating from troubled Haiti en route to the southern reaches of the United States of America (Villiers, 1994; Frelick, 1993; Motomura, 1993; Jones, 1995, 1996). An intrinsic part of that program was the establishment of offshore processing centres for determining whether boat people have 'colourable' claims for refugee status. The most wellknown of these centres was established at Guantanamo Bay, a US Trust territory on the Island of Cuba." The US arrangements have a number of features that are echoed in the Pacific Solution — among them the denial of access to US refugee status determination procedures and to the US judicial system (Lowenstein International Human Rights Clinic, 1993). The US policy was more extreme than anything envisioned by Australia. At the height of the outflow from Haiti, the American coastguard abandoned any pretext at all at screening the fugitives for refugee claims (Frelick, 1993).

It is my view that Australia has modeled itself quite consciously on its US ally to bolster its immunity from (official) international legal criticism. It must be said that, from the perspective of international politics, the alignment in state practice between Australia and the United States has been successful.

The *Tampa* Affair and Australia's Domestic Immigration Laws

Interesting parallels emerge also between the way the Australian courts responded to the ' *Tampa* Affair' and the American judiciary's response to the Haitian interdiction program. In both Australia and the United States, public interest advocates came forward to challenge the policies and practices adopted by the respective governments to block the admission of boat people. The action in the United States went all the way to the US Supreme Court. With one powerful dissent (Sale v Haitian Centers Council Inc, 1993; Blackmun, 1994), the action resulted in a ruling that the interdiction program was legal because the prohibition on refoulement did not operate in respect of actions taken outside of US territory — in this case on the High Seas.

In Australia, challenges made to the Government's actions in the *Tampa* Affair also failed. The Government's refusal to allow any access to the persons taken on board the *Tampa* meant that advocates in

Australia were unable to gain instructions from the rescuees for the purpose of mounting a legal challenge under the Migration Act 1958 (Cth). The applicants were acknowledged as having standing to bring an action for orders in the nature of habeas corpus so as to seek the release of the *Tampa* rescuees, but were held to have no right to mount any other kind of legal challenge.[14] The advocates succeeded at first instance before North J in the Federal Court, who held that the asylum seekers were being detained by the Australian authorities in circumstances where there was no basis in Australian law for the action being taken (Victorian Council for Civil Liberties v Minister, 2001 at 490). On appeal, a majority of the Full Federal Court overturned these rulings. French J, with whom Beaumont J agreed, relied on the reasoning of the High Court in an earlier attempt to challenge the lawfulness of a regime mandating the detention of asylum seekers within Australia (Chu Kheng Lim v Minister, 1992; Crock, 1993). Somewhat counter-intuitively, he held that the rescuees were not being 'detained' at law because they were free to travel anywhere they wished (except to Australia) (Vadarlis v Ruddock, 2001 at 548). His Honour went further to suggest that the nature of the executive power conferred on the government under the Australian Constitution may be such that legislation is not needed to render lawful any actions taken to protect Australia's borders.

Amidst the flurry of legislative change on 26 September 2001, French J's comments did not go unnoticed by government drafters. The Migration Act amendments included a new s7A, which confirms the power of the Executive to act outside of any legislative authority. The new section reads:

> The existence of a statutory power under this Act does not prevent the exercise of any executive power of the Commonwealth to protect Australia's borders, including, where necessary, by ejecting persons who have crossed those borders.

In referring to 'persons', the Act makes no distinction between citizens and foreigners.

In his judgement, Beaumont J held that the action had to fail because there was no 'relevant substantive cause of action (that is, a legal right) recognised by law and enforceable by (the) court'. He held that the Federal Court had no inherent jurisdiction to issue a writ of habeas corpus[15] and that, in any event, a writ to force release from detention could not be used to compel the government to admit an individual onto

Australian territory. His Honour held that the executive alone has 'power to authorise such an entry'.

Taken to its logical conclusion, this last aspect of Beaumont J's ruling sits curiously with the long tradition of judicial review of immigration applications in Australia. Prior to the introduction of the current regulatory scheme in immigration, no applicant for a visa or entry permit could lay claim to a 'right' to enter the country. However, this fact did not prevent the Australian courts from entertaining any number of challenges to visa refusals, from persons both outside Australia and within the country.[16]

Leaving aside the correctness or otherwise of his reasoning, Beaumont J's judgment in the *Tampa* case is interesting in the wider context of the affair. The judgment is replete with a sense of urgency, if not moral panic. The judge underscores passages and words. His conclusion — that an alien has no right to enter Australia — is placed quite literally in bold print. The effect is to emphasis and reemphasize the outsider status of the rescuees. The word 'alien' appears no less than 27 times in the 30 paragraphs of his judgment.

None of the judges in the appeal court mention the tumultuous events that occurred in America on the day North J handed down his ruling — September 11 2001. As the world came to learn about Osama Bin Laden, Al Qaeda and the Taliban in Afghanistan, it was no time at all before Australia's politicians were warning a frightened public that the Afghan and Middle Eastern boat people 'could be terrorists'. One is left to wonder whether Beaumont J would have been quite as vehement absent '911'.

The tonal change between the primary judgment and the appeal rulings could not be more marked. Of the four Federal Court judges, North J at first instance is the only one to spend much time describing the rescuees, identifying them as fugitives from Afghanistan who 'it is probable ... are people genuinely fearing persecution'. Dissenting in the Full Court, Black CJ agreed with the substance of North J's rulings. However, his carefully reasoned judgment sticks closely to legal principle, assiduously avoiding any emotive descriptions of the people behind the action. Beaumont J's postscript does acknowledge the potential that the rescuees could be refugees, but his addendum underscores (again, quite literally), the international nature of the legal obligation not to refoule refugees. His Honour draws attention to the fact that what became known as the 'Pacific Solution' did not involve the refoulement of the rescuees: that all would have their asylum claims assessed outside of Australia.

The emphasis on Australia's domestic immigration laws in the *Tampa* action in the Federal Court highlights the relative insignificance of international law in the scheme of Australia's reactions throughout the affair. Australia has no Bill of Rights or other overriding standard operating to protect human rights. Unlike Britain and the countries of the European Union, there is no external forum to which an appeal might be made invoking principles of international law.

Island Refuge or Castaways? The 'Pacific Solution'

The absence of adequate accountability mechanisms at law emerges just as forcefully in the second stage of the ' *Tampa* Affair'. There are aspects of the socalled Pacific Solution that are ripe for criticism — not the least in the apparent disregard for local human rights standards in those two countries.[17] However, from the perspective of refugee law, once again it is difficult to assert categorically that the initiatives taken were and are in breach of international law.

As noted earlier, there are many aspects of the so-called 'Pacific Solution' that find resonance in United States policy and practice. It is difficult to imagine America 'excising' parts of its offshore territories. However, the United States has established detention centres and holding camps in some of its 'trust' territories and protectorates. It has also enacted different legal regimes for persons detained away from its mainland territories (Musalo, Moore & Boswell, 1997). One notable feature of the US legislation is the provisions reducing or removing altogether the right of noncitizens apprehended in this way to access America's administrative law systems.[18] A key aspect of the 'Pacific Solution' was to replicate this situation in Australia, removing the right of refugee claimants to appeal against adverse decisions to an administrative tribunal; removing access to both lawyers and judicial review (DIMIA, 2002).

The arrangements on Nauru and on Manus Island in Papua New Guinea are not sustainable. Indeed, every indication is that the measures were taken as a short term solution to the panic surrounding the *Tampa* affair and its aftermath. The IOM and UNHCR have politely declined to take on the processing of any more boat people apprehended in the Pacific region en route for Australia. It is unlikely that other Pacific Islands will agree to take on processing for Australia (Oxfam &

Community Aid Abroad, 2002). If there is a future for the Pacific Solution, it lies in the detention facility planned for Christmas Island: this is to be Australia's Guantanamo Bay.

Australia's justification for these arrangements again lies in the argument that the boat people seeking to find refuge in Australia are 'secondary flow' refugees, if they meet the UN definition of refugee at all (UN, 1999). Once more, various arguments are made as to why the minimalist conditions for both the detention and processing of the asylum seekers are consistent with international legal obligations. First, a conscious effort appears to have been made to ensure that Nauru and Manus Island conformed with (no more and no less than) the minimum requirements established by the United Nations in its front-line relief operations in cases of large-scale refugee flows. The rationale is that 'secondary flow' refugees should not be able to gain a procedural advantage by their forum shopping activities. Minister Ruddock has drawn attention to the inequity implicit in the fact that asylum seekers who access Australia's refugee determination processes are many times more likely to gain recognition as refugees than are those processed by UNHCR in its front line field operations (Crosweller & Saunders, 2002). As well as being unfair to those 'screened out' by UNHCR, the elaborate systems of countries like Australia are decried as magnets that encourage asylum seekers to bypass the 'regular' refugee management processes.

The implication of UNHCR and of IOM in the 'Pacific Solution' gives credence to this rather formalistic vision of the world's refugee problem and what should be done to resolve it. Whether UNHCR and IOM are happy with the situation to which they are party, however, is quite another question. My discussions with UNHCR in Canberra lead me to believe that UNHCR would have been happy to allow the *Tampa* asylum seekers access to legal advice and that it was Australia's opposition that lead to the closure of the Island state to would-be refugee advocates (telephone conversation between author and Ms Ellen Hansen of UNHCR, March 2002).

While the *Tampa* rescuees taken in by New Zealand fared well," the arrangements on Nauru and Manus Island raise a variety of issues about compliance with the Rule of Law — and arguably create more problems than they have solved. From the perspective of the Refugee Convention, arguments could be raised that the arrangements on Nauru and Manus Island constitute a penalty on refugees contrary to Article 31 of the

Convention. It is worth noting in this context that Nauru is not a party to the Refugee Convention, while Papua New Guinea has signed but made a number of reservations.²⁰ From the perspective of the domestic laws of both Nauru and Papua New Guinea, the establishment of the detention facilities, and the indefinite incarceration of the asylum seekers without judicial oversight is questionable. Both Nauru and Papua New Guinea are countries with Bills of Rights that prohibit arbitrary detention.²¹ Put simply, the financial inducements of the Australian Government have resulted in both instances in the establishment of facilities that, at the very least, sit uneasily with the human rights regimes of the host governments.

'The Australian Government has played word games when speaking of the Pacific Solution arrangements. As Frank Brennan SJ notes:

> The Minister's first defence is to claim that the facilities in those places (Nauru and Manus Island) are not detention centres despite the Migration Legislation Amendment (Transitional Movement) Act 2002 speaking of 'the detention of the person in a country in respect of which a declaration is in force (s198D(3)(c)). And the bills digest for the Migration Legislation Amendment (Transitional Movement) Bill 2002 speaks of the removal of persons 'to a place such as a "Pacific Solution" detention facility on Nauru or Papua New Guinea'.

Even Senator George Brandis and Mr John Hodges in the Senate Select Committee on a certain Maritime Incident have referred to the 'detention centres' in those places and the 'detainees' kept therein. In his evidence on 1 May 2002, Mr Hodges said, 'Nauru is by far the worst of the detention centres' (2002:13).

The Australian Government has done its best to distance itself from criticisms of the way the camps are being run and of the conditions in the camps. Interestingly, these efforts do not appear to have succeeded in deflecting criticisms of the Nauru and Papua New Guinea facilities as manifestations of Australian policy.

Leaving aside the extent to which the Pacific Solution represents a breach of international law, the costs of the exercise to Australia in financial terms have been considerable. According to the Minister's press releases, four year funding for the operation costs of offshore processing has been estimated at $129.3 million for 2002³, with an additional $270 million allocated for construction and operating costs for facilities on Christmas Island (and CocosKeeling Is) (Ruddock, 2002). As the Refugee Council of Australia (2002) has noted, the budget allocations of $2.8 billion over four years represent expenditure in the vicinity of $700,000 for each of a nominal 4,000 asylum seekers who may come to Australia by boat during that period.

The Nauruan Government has been paid or pledged $30 million for the financial year of 20012.[22] The arrangements in Papua New Guinea are reported to have cost in excess of $24 million, with the number of asylum seekers a mere 446 (ABC Radio, 2001; Oxfam & Community Aid Abroad, 2002:10). In practical terms, what Australia did was to use the interdicted asylum seekers as barter for massive increases in aid payments to both countries. In the case of Papua New Guinea, the decision to trade refugees for Australian aid has not gained popular support. Indeed, some have suggested that the policy contributed to the dramatic decline in the fortunes of the governing Peoples' Democratic Movement party, perhaps contributing to the precipitous decision of Prime Minister Sir Mekere Morauta to resign before the completion of the elections in August 2002. Australia, some would argue, has emerged from the affair as a regional bully, using its financial muscle to force struggling countries to do its dirty work.

As the refugee claims of the asylum seekers on Nauru and Manus Island are processed, interesting issues emerge when the processing data released by UNHCR and by DIMIA are compared. The official statistics released by UNHCR on 31 July 2002 in respect of its Nauru determinations suggest that Iraqi asylum seekers on Nauru have been accepted at the rate of 84 per cent. The data released by DIMIA in May 2002 for Iraqis on Nauru shows Australia's approval at around 53 per cent. The recognition rates for Iraqis on Manus Island as of 20 May 2002 were around 76 per cent. As DIMIA has not released statistics with the same breakdown as UNHCR, it is difficult to follow exactly what is going on. However, the available data suggests that UNHCR processing is more generous than that of the Australian authorities on Nauru and Papua New Guinea. Indeed, on the face of things, UNHCR processing appears to be in line with the processing of Iraqis in Australia (including appeals to the Refugee Review Tribunal), which results in approvals of Iraqis claimants at well over 80 per cent. This is interesting as one of the stated rationales of the Pacific Solution is that the Australian onshore processing system is too generous, relative to standards set by UNHCR. Minister Ruddock's claim in late 2001 was that an Iraqi asylum seeker was 'six times more likely' to gain recognition in Australia than through UNHCR processes. In the case of asylum seekers on Nauru and Manus

Island, the statistics supplied by UNHCR — although not those emanating from the Government — suggest that processing by UNHCR was, in fact, more likely to result in the recognition of claims than processing by the Australian authorities.

UNHCR Refugee Status Determinations Nauru - 31 July 2002								
Nationality	Total No. Persons	Accept 1st Instance	Rejected 1st Instance	Accept Appeal	Reject Appeal	Pending	Vol Repatra'n	Acceptce Rate #
Iraqi	201	126	75	36	31	8		84%
Palestinian	27	14	13	10	3			89%
Afghan	292*	32	244			239	5	12% #
Pakistani	3						3	0%
Sri Lankan	6		5	2	3		1	40%
Total	**529**	**172**	**339**	**46**	**37**	**247**	**9**	**43%**
Note:	* 14 Afghans were resettled to New Zealand without receiving a determination							
	* 2 Afghans chose to repatriate without receiving a determination							
	# Acceptance rate is calculated as a percentage of decisions (not counting pending cases & voluntary repatriation without determination). This is of particular note in the large number of pending decisions for the Afghan caseload.							
	131 Afghans from the Tampa went to New Zealand for RSD							
	1 Afghan from the Tampa was processed by DIMIA due to family links							
Resettlement:	59 departed to New Zealand							
	5 departed to Australia							
	9 accepted by Sweden, not yet departed							

Australian government refugee determinations Decisions Handed Down on Nauru – MPS 41/2002 – 30 May 2002					
	Iraqi		Other Nationalities		Total
	Approved	Refused	Approved	Refused	
Decisions handed down week commencing 27.5.02	10	49	3	0	62
Decisions previously handed down - Australia - UNHCR	60 126	12 75	0 21	7 22	79 244
Total	**196**	**136**	**24**	**29**	**385**

Australian government refugee determinations Decisions Handed Down on Manus Island – MPS 39/2002 – 23 May 2002					
	Iraqi		Other Nationalities		Total
	Approved	Refused	Approved	Refused	
Decisions handed down week commencing 20.5.02	115	56	7	11	189
Decisions previously handed down	101	12	3	0	116
Total	216	68	10	11	305

Landfall at Last? The Plight of 'Unauthorised' Refugees and 'Transitional Movement' Persons in Australia

The issue of who is to take those people processed on Nauru and Manus Island and recognised as refugees is an enduring problem. The tiny Island of Nauru has made it plain from the outset that it will not accept any of the *Tampa* or Acheng refugees for permanent resettlement. Papua New Guinea is also not well placed to take refugees for resettlement. New Zealand and Sweden have accepted some refugees, but Australia has been reluctant to follow suit. Although it has accepted 42 refugees from Manus Island, as of 1 July 2002, it had only taken one refugee from Nauru. This is in spite of the fact that fully half of the refugees first recognised by UNHCR on Nauru are reputed to have relatives of some sort in Australia (conversation between author and Ms Ellen Hansen, UNHCR, March 2002).

The dilemma facing the Pacific Solution refugees highlights once again the limits of the international protection regime on the one hand and the iniquity of Australia's policies, on the other. The bottom line is that UNHCR cannot force countries to accept refugees. Its Executive Committee has examined the problems associated with the dislocation of refugees' families. In that Committee's Conclusion No 24, UNHCR has called upon state parties to the Convention to make the reunification of refugee families a first priority (UNHCR, 1981). In Australia, the public response of at least one senior Departmental official has been to reject ExCom Conclusion No. 24 as 'not relevant' to the issue of Australia's legal obligations (Discussion between author and Mr Robert Illingsworth, Deputy Secretary Refugee Policy Branch, DIMIA, 2 April 2002).

There is a special irony in Australia's unwillingness to take the Pacific Solution refugees. While the assertion cannot be proved, there is some evidence that, absent changes to Australian laws in 1999, many of the refugees on Nauru and Manus Island would never have had to resort to the people smugglers and their boats to seek safe haven in the first place.

Until 1999 when the first Border Protection Act 1999 (Cth) was passed, all noncitizens recognised as refugees in Australia were treated in the same way. All received permanent residence, with all the entitlements flowing from that status. In that year changes to the Migration Regulations meant that boat people and other unauthorised arrivals would no longer gain access to permanent residence or to the attendant rights to (legal) family reunion. These provisions were introduced in spite of (or perhaps, because of) the fact that more boat people were gaining recognition as refugees in 1999 than in any other time in Australian history. The almost immediate result was to change the usual pattern of boatpeople behaviour. The common practice was to send the male (head) of the family by boat to find safe haven, using the people smugglers as gobetween. That way, the father would suffer the rigours and perils of the sea voyage and the women and children would follow in due course using the regular immigration mechanisms. The inability to sponsor family has forced refugee families away from the regular migration channel and into the arms of the people smugglers. If families do not use the people smugglers, the present system in Australia means that they could well face permanent separation. The change is reflected in the composition of the detention centre population. In 1999 the number of children in custody leapt from 5 per cent to 34 per cent in the space of a month.

With the passage of the Migration Legislation Amendment (Transitional Movement) Act 2002, the Government has attempted to cement its vision of refugee processing with legislation that allows people processed offshore to be brought to Australia without gaining any rights to apply for a visa or to challenge their detention. For most purposes, individuals brought to Australia under this legislation are treated as though they are not here. For those who have family in Australia, this represents particular problems.

Although nominally being processed outside of Australian law, asylum seekers on Nauru and Manus Island are probably subjected to the same refugee law standards as are used for refugee claimants within

Australia. Although Australia has never moved to enact the UN definition into its migration laws, on 26 September 2001 the Migration Act was amended so as to 'clarify' — or, rather, constrain — the way Australian decision makers are supposed to read the UN definition of refugee. The amended legislation directs that families cannot be regarded as a 'particular social group' for the purposes of the definition. Put simply, it is no longer permissible to take into account persecution suffered by one family member when determining the claim of another in the family: each applicant must meet the definition in her or his own right. For women and children, the changes mean that their refugee claims will fail unless they have a political profile of their own or they are with their husbands or fathers at the time of applying.

At the end of January 2002 there were 48 groups of women and children in Woomera detention centre with husbands on the outside who had come on earlier boats and who had gained recognition as refugees. Where the women's claims are rejected, the only solution seems to be for the refugee husbands to go to the Minister personally to get permission to lodge another refugee application, this time including the wives and children. In the meantime the women and children face removal and/or they languish in detention.

For those outside of Australia, however, this is not an option. The husbands and fathers in Australia (and recognised as refugees) cannot lodge fresh refugee applications so as to include their family on the one form. Moreover, once rejected, the family offshore cannot be helped, even if they are brought to Australia in transit under the Transitional Movement provisions. In these cases, the refugee fathers and husbands will have two options. They will either have to throw in their attempt to find safe haven, returning with their families to face persecution. Or they will be forced to stand by and watch as their families are returned without them. As 'voluntary' returnees, Australia could avoid the direct charge of refouling the refugee fathers and husbands. Whether this scenario is in keeping with the spirit, rather than the letter, of the Refugee Convention is highly questionable.

Conclusion

Questions remain about what exactly caused Australia to react as it did in August 2001. Conspiracy theories that assert the whole affair was orchestrated for political ends cannot provide the whole answer. Assertions that Australia is a racist society, locked in a protectionist and alarmist mindset by its refusal to face the ghosts of its white supremacist past also tend to result in caricature, rather than characterisation. 2001 was an election year and the way the government of the day played events undoubtedly did contribute to its electoral victory. It is my view that the *Tampa* Affair did have its roots in deep Australian culture and that a culture of fear, isolationism, xenophobia. However, it was also an event — or series of events — carved out at a particularly fraught moment in human history. It should be recalled that the first instance decision of North J in the *Tampa* litigation was handed down only hours before the first plane hit the World Trade Centre in New York on 11 September 2001. While the complexity of the causative factors may not exonerate Australia or excuse the ongoing delicts of its refugee policies, it is well to acknowledge that the Affair cannot be adequately explained in the two-minute grabs favoured by the modern media.

First of all, there is something about boat people that excites extraordinary reactions in people. In this, Australia is far from unique. Perhaps it is a primordial fear of invading hordes. Perhaps it is that water borders are more obvious than land borders, making territorial incursions from the sea more keenly felt. Certainly, the constant talk of numbers cannot help: '20 million of concern to UNHCR'; 'more on the move than in any other time of human history'. Mention has been made of America's Haitian interdiction program and of the extreme lengths to which the United States has gone to prevent seafaring asylum seekers from landing on its territory. Less extreme examples of countries reacting to the arrival or threatened arrival of 'boat people' abound. In many instances the responses are quite disproportionate to the threats posed by the unwanted arrivals. For example, in 1999, rumours that a boat may be making its way to New Zealand lead to the enactment of immigration detention laws (Immigration Act, 1987:s128(13B); Haines, 2000). Even compassionate Canada has responded with unusual defensiveness when faced with the arrival of boats carrying asylum seekers (Kumin, 2000).

Putting to one side the invasion fears, the second complicating factor is the complexity of the people smuggling story. The asylum seekers who arrive by boat in Australia, as in other parts of the world, do so using the offices of 'people smugglers'. As well as implicating the fugitives in criminal and often highly exploitative activities, the people smugglers help to blur the line between asylum seeker and migrant. As the Australian government is quick to emphasise, the boat people arriving in Australia are very rarely coming directly from the country in which they fear persecution. In most cases, they have travelled through a variety of countries. Sometimes they have tried to find refuge in the countries they passed through; sometimes their voyage has been more or less direct. There is often a grain of truth in even the most alarmist rhetoric in those seeking to vilify the asylum seeker.

The use of leaky boats as the vehicle for conveying refugees to Australia must be a matter of concern and something to discourage — if only to ensure no more tragedies like the one that saw 370 people lose their lives off the Indonesian coast in late November 2001. However, it is equally clear that the 'Pacific Solution' is no solution to people smuggling. While there are families striving to be reunited; while there are people caught in limbo yearning for a safe haven, the refugees will continue to batter at Australia's door. It is no solution to decry the refugee's efforts to save themselves and their families, to vilify the victims who take the initiative to struggle against the oppression in their lives. It is no solution to adopt policies that perpetuate and exacerbate suffering in the name of 'control' and deterrence.

The Australian Defence force personnel have shown us in their courageous denunciation of the lies told about asylum seekers rescued at sea during the '*Tampa*' election of 2001 that Truth can triumph in a democracy like Australia. None-the-less, I cannot but reflect on how easily we can be persuaded of the inhumanity of people in positions of great vulnerability. 'What kind of person ', we asked ourselves, 'would throw their children overboard; would sew shut the lips of their children?' 'We would not want people like that to live with people like us, would we?' The Australian media have at last begun to show us that they, the refugees, after all, are not so unlike us. Australia's policies are not alright. They are not in compliance with our international legal obligations. They are un-Australian.

REFERENCES

Australian Broadcasting Corporation (ABC Radio) (2001), 'Locals question benefits of adopting 'Pacific Solution'', Asia Pacific program, Nov 2001.

Australian Broadcasting Corporation (ABC TV) (2002), 'To Deter and To Deny', Four Corners, March 2002.

Australian Labor Party (ALP), (2000), *2000 Platform and Constitution*, http://www.australianpolitics.com/parties/alp/policy/pl atform2000.pdf.

Blackmun, H.A. (1994), 'The Supreme Court and the Law of Nations', *Yale Law Journal*, 104, 3949.

Brennan, F. (2002), 'Developing Just Refugee Policies in Australia: Local, National and International Concerns', University of Sydney, 7 Aug 2002, unpublished paper.

Button, J. (2002), 'Beyond Belief: What Future for Labor?, Quarterly Essay, 6. 179

Chu Kheng Lim v Minister for Immigration and Ethnic Affairs (1992), 176 CLR 1.

Churchill, R.R. & Lowe, A.V. (1999), *The Law of the Sea*, 3rd Edition. Juris Publishing: Manchester.

Conyngham v Minister (Platters' Case) (1986), 68 ALR 441.

Crock, M. (1993), 'Climbing Jacob's Ladder: The High Court and the Administrative Detention of Asylum Seekers in Australia', *Sydney Law Review*, 15, 338356.

Crock, M. (2001), 'Echoes of the Old Countries or Brave New Worlds? Legal responses to refugees and Asylum Seekers in Australia and New Zealand, *Revue québécoise de droit international*, 14(1), 55.

Crosweller, A. & Saunders, M. (2002), 'Refugees plight a "lifestyle choice"', *The Australian*, 8 Jan 2002, p. 2.

Department of Immigration, Multicultural and Indigenous Affairs (DIMIA) (2002), 'Offshore Processing Arrangements', Fact Sheet No. 76, 2 Jan 2002.

Fallon, J.E. (1991), 'Federal Policy and U.S. Territories: the Political Restructuring of the United States of America', *Pacific Affairs*, 64, 2341.

Fonteyne, JP. (2001), 'All Adrift in a Sea of Illegitimacy: An International Law Perspective on the *Tampa* Affair', *Public Law Review*, 12(4), 249253.

Frelick, B. (1993), 'Haitian boat interdiction: First asylum and first principles of refugee protection', *Cornell International Law Journal*, 26, 675695.

GoodwinGill, G. (1996), *The Refugee in International Law*, 2nd Edition. Oxford University Press: Oxford.

GoodwinGill, G. (2001), 'Article 31 of the 1951 Convention relating to the Status of Refugees: Non Penalisation, Detention and Protection', in E. Feller, V. Türk & F. Nicholson (Ed.), *Refugee Protection in International Law*. UNHCR and Cambridge University Press: Cambridge.

Haines, R. (2000), 'An Overview of Refugee Law in New Zealand: Background and Current Issues', Inaugural Meeting of International Association of Refugee Law Judges, 10 Mar 2000. [Available at http://www.refugee.org.nz/IARLJ3-00Haines.html].

Hancock, N. (20012a), 'Border Protection (Validation and Enforcement Powers) Bill 2001 (Cth)', *Bills Digest* No. 62 2 0 0 1 2. [Available at http://www.aph.gov.au/library/pubs/bd/2001 02/02bd062.htm].

Hancock, N. (20012b), 'Refugee Law — Recent Legislative Developments', Current Issues Brief 5 20012. [Available at http://www.aph.gov.au/library/pubs/cib/2001 02/02cib05.htm].

Hathaway, J.C. (2001), 'Immigration Law is Not Refugee Law' (pp. 3947), in US Committee for Refugees (Ed.), World Refugee Survey, 2001. USCR: Washington, D.C.

Jones, T.D. (1995), 'A Human Rights Tragedy: the Cuban and Haitian refugee crises revisited', *Georgetown Immigration Law Review*, 29(3), 479523.

Jones, T.D. (1996), 'International Decision', *American Journal of International Law*, 90(3), 477483.

Kumin, J. (2000), 'Between Sympathy and Anger: How Open Will Canada's Door be?', in US Committee for Refugees (Ed.), *World Refugee Survey*. [Available at www.refugees.org/world/articles/wrs00_sympathy.htm].

Lowenstein International Human Rights Clinic (1993), 'Aliens and the Duty of Nonrefoulement: Haitian Centers Council v McNary', *Harvard Human Rights Journal*, 6, 128.

Meron, T. (1995), 'Extraterritoriality of Human Rights Treaties', *American Journal of International Law*, 89(1), 7882.

Minister for Immigration and Multicultural Affairs v Ibrahim (2000), HCA 55 (16 November 2000).

Motomura, H. (1993), 'Haitian Asylum Seekers: Interdiction and Immigrants' Rights', *Cornell International Law Journal*, 26, 695717.

Musalo, K., Gibson, L., Knight, S. & Taylor, E. (2001), 'The Expedited Removal study: Report On The First Three Years Of Implementation Of Expedited Removal', *Notre Dame Journal of Law, Ethics & Public Policy*, 15(1), 130145.

Musalo, K., Moore, J. & Boswell, R. (1997), *Refugee Law and Policy: Cases and Materials*. Carolina Academic Press: USA.

O'Connell, D. P. (1984) *The International Law of the Sea*, Volume II (I. Shearer, Ed.). Claredon Press: Oxford.

Oxfam & Community Aid Abroad (2002), 'Adrift in the Pacific: The Implications of Australia's Pacific Refugee Solution', March 2002. [Available at http://www.caa.org.au/campaigns/submissions/pacificso lution/]

Pugash, J. (1977), 'The Dilemma of the Sea Refugee: Rescue Without Refuge', *Harvard International Law Journal*, 18(3), 577604.

Re Officer in Charge of cells, ACT Supreme Court; Ex parte Eastman (1994), 123 ALR 478.

Refugee Council of Australia (2002), 'Reflections on the 20023 Budget'. [Available at http://www.justrefugeeprograms.com.au/news/Newsfra meset.htm]

Rothwell, D. (2002), 'The Law of the Sea and the MV *Tampa* Incident: Reconciling Maritime Principles with Coastal State Sovereignty', *Public Law Review*, 13, 118-127.

Ruddock, P. (2002), 'Offshore Processing Developments and Related Savings', MPS 33/2002, 14 May, 2002. Sale v Haitian Centers Council Inc (1993), 509 US 155. Schaeffer, R.P. (197880), 'The Singular Plight of Seaborne Refugees', *Australian Yearbook of International Law*, 8, 213234.

Shearer, I. (1997), 'Jurisdiction' (pp. 161192), in S. Blay, R. Piotrowicz & B.M. Tsamenyi (Eds.), *Public International Law: An Australian Perspective*. Oxford University Press: Melbourne.

Tauman, J. (2002), 'Rescued at Sea, but Nowhere to Go: The Cloudy Legal Waters of the *Tampa* Crisis', *Pacific Rim Law and Policy Journal*, 11(2), 461496.

UN (1999), Draft Protocol against the Smuggling of Migrants by Land, Air and Sea, Supplementing the United Nations Convention against Transnational Organized Crime, 13 May 1999, A/AC.254/4/Add.1/Rev.1.

UNHCR (1981), ExCom Conclusion No. 24 (XXXII) — Family reunification. Vadarlis v Ruddock (2001), 110 FCR 491.

Victorian Council for Civil Liberties and Ors v Minister for Immigration, Multiculturalism and Indigenous Affairs (2001), 110 FCR 452.

Villiers, J.D. (1994), 'Closed Borders, Closed Ports: the plight of Haitians seeking political asylum in the United States', *Brooklyn Law Review*, 60(3), 841928.

ENDNOTES

1. For another account of the events surrounding the *Tampa*'s rescue mission see Hathaway, 2001:3947.
2. To these other areas of law could be added. The affair also raised issues of mercantile law, as the *Tampa* was a commercial cargo vessel. For a discussion of the incident within the context of constitutional and human rights law, see the special issue devoted to the affair in (2002) 13 Public Law Review.
3. The case was taken on appeal to the Full Federal Court. See Vadarlis v Ruddock (2001). Leave to appeal to the High Court was refused.
4. This is the term coined by North J in the Federal Court in the litigation brought by public interest advocates in the *Tampa* Affair. His Honour explained his choice of word as an attempt to find a neutral (and nonemotive) term to describe the people at the heart of the incident. See Victorian Council for Civil Liberties and Ors v Minister (2001:457, para 17).
5. Flying Fish Cove on Christmas Island is not rated to dock a vessel with the dimensions of the *Tampa*. The Immigration Department's Mr Robert Illingsworth asserts that *Tampa* Captain Arne Rinnan was obliged to keep the ship under power during the standoff with the Australian authorities.
6. The Afghanis on board the *Tampa* made their intentions clear to the Norwegian ambassador who visited the ship at its Christmas Island mooring. See Hathaway (2001:39).
7. Most of the *Tampa* rescuees were Afghani nationals. Before the US intervention in Afghanistan lead to the defeat of the ruling Taliban in late 2001, over 80 per cent of Afghan asylum seekers in Australia were gaining recognition as refugees. Of the 130 *Tampa* asylum seekers accepted by New Zealand, all but one were recognised at first instance as refugees and offered permanent resettlement.
8. Tauman provides examples some of the more egregious instances of humanitarian neglect, amongst them the tragedies of the St Louis — which resulted in the ultimate death of 907 refugees from Nazi Germany; of the *Struma* where 769 Romanian Jews were left to drown; and ofthe Vietnamese boat people who were left by a United States naval vessel to die of starvation in the South China Seas. See Tauman (2002:4612, 4923).

9. For a discussion of the legislative changes 'excising' certain offshore territories from Australia's migration zone see Crock (2001:8082).
10. This underscores the assertions made by the Australian Government about the lawfulness of its actions. On this point, see also Meron (1995:801).
11. See Border Protection (Validation and Enforcement Powers) Act 2001 (Cth); Migration Amendment (Excision from Migration Zone) (Consequential Provisions) Act 2 0 0 1 (Cth); Migration Legislation Amendment Act (No 1) 2001; Migration Legislation Amendment Act (No 3) 2001; Migration Legislation Amendment Act (No 5) 2001; Migration Legislation Amendment Act (No 6) 2001; and Migration (Judicial Review) Act 2001 (Cth). These measures were opposed only by the Democrats, the Greens and independent Senator Brian Harradine.
12. This characterisation of the refugees is underscored by the Government by removing one place in Australia's overseas 'humanitarian' intake for every asylum seeker recognised as a refugee in Australia.
13. This facility became known as Camp XRay in late 2001, after being converted into a holding facility for persons taken prison in Afghanistan during the early stages of the US 'War against Terrorism'. Other such centres have been established at the other US trust territories in the Pacific. See, for example, Fallon (1991).
14. The Applicants failed in their attempt to argue that the Government was obliged by the Migration Act to land the rescuees. Eric Vardarlis argued that the status of the rescuees as unlawful non–citizens demanded that they be taken into immigration detention within Australia pursuant to s189. The other applicants argued that s245F of this Act required the Government to bring the rescuees to the mainland of Australia, where they would then be entitled to lodge formal claims for refugee status pursuant to s36 of the Act. A writ of mandamus was sought to compel the Minister to perform his statutory duty. Eric Vardarlis also argued that the refusal to allow him access to the rescuees constituted a breach of his implied constitutional freedom of communication. He sought an injunction and mandamus to allow him to give legal advice to the rescuees.
15. His Honour cited Re Officer in Charge of Cells, ACT Supreme Court; Ex parte Eastman (1994) where the High Court held that

habeas corpus could not be used as a means of collaterally impeaching the correctness of orders made by a court of competent jurisdiction that had not been shown to be a nullity. In that case the High Court also held that the High Court's jurisdiction to entertain this writ could only arise as an incident of an action brought within the court's original jurisdiction. See Beaumont J at paras 1023.

16. True that the courts have been loathed to order grant of a visa, rather than order reconsideration of legal decision. See Conyngham v Minister (Platters' Case) (1986).

17. See below, n 21.

18. See Refugee Act 1980, Pub L No 96212, 94 Stat 107 (1980), 8USC para 1253(h) (1988), amending para 243(h) of the Immigration and Nationality Act. Note that moves were also made to restrict the access of illegal entrants to appeal and judicial review mechanisms. See Illegal Immigration Reform and Immigrant Responsibility Act 1996; and Musalo, Gibson, Knight & Taylor, (2001).

19. New Zealand had its quota of 131 asylum seekers processed within weeks of arrival. In January 2002, all but one had gained recognition as refugees and were granted permanent residence in New Zealand. See Oxfam & Community Aid Abroad (2002).

20. PNG does not accept the following Convention obligations: paid employment (art 17); housing (art 21); public education (art 22); freedom of movement (art 26); nondiscrimination against refugees who enter illegally (art 31); expulsion (art 32); and naturalisation (art 34).

21. For the Nauruan Constitution, see Part II, Protection of Fundamental Rights and Freedoms, art 3:
http://www.vanuatu.usp.ac.fj/paclawmat/Nauru_legislation/Nauru_Constitution.html; and for the Constitution of Papua New Guinea, see the Preamble and Art 42 (Liberty of the Person):
http://www.vanuatu.usp.ac.fj/paclawmat/PNG_legislation/Constitution.htm.

22. For a description of how this money is to be spent, see Oxfam Report (2002:13).

CHAPTER FOUR

WHY AREN'T THERE ANY FLOWERS IN AUSTRALIA?

FRAN GALE AND MICHAEL DUDLEY

'All I can see is the wire and us behind it' three year old Rias said, staring out, through wire palisade fencing, across the desert.

Not only is the visibility and worldview of detained children, such as Rias, constricted with little sense of future or hope; the inhumane conditions in which detained children live are not visible to the community at large.

Locked up behind two high walls of razor wire in compounds, which are barren, harsh areas of dust and stones with no shade, children in Woomera and other desert detention centres endure their daytoday lives incarcerated. Behind high razor wire walls in city detention centres children follow guards using keycards to unlock three or four doors to reach a visitors' room.

Often subdued by defensive management and tranquilising drugs such as Valium, children and young people in detention have their 'voice' silenced. Not uncommonly, they are referred to by numbers rather than names. Having no names, having no voice, the children's humanity becomes obscured.

Access to detainees in immigration detention is limited and independent observers have great difficulty getting inside centers such as Woomera (PAHASC, 2002:29). High barbed wire walls, guards and restriction to a particular 'visitor area' confront visitors. As Justice Marcus Einfeld observes '(politicians) … close off the camps to the media and to visitors so nobody knows what's going on inside … They don't tell people the truth' (Banham, 2002:3).

The advanced democratic state claims transparency for its public institutions yet no transparency for detention institutions is even claimed. There are few formalised processes of legal and professional accountability. This exacerbates the invisibility of detained children and young people.

Official discourse insists on the well being of children and young people in Australian immigration detention (Taylor, 2002). However, no screening or assessment of detained children's needs takes place in Australian detention centres. This adds another layer of invisibility. Moreover, young detainees are often invisible in official discourse because they are subsumed within families who in turn are subsumed under the category 'asylum seekers'.

Invisibility of children in detention is also reflected in the analysis of children's needs in the broader literature. There is little comprehensive information about the emotional and social well being of asylum seeking children and young people in detention. The absence of information is in part a reflection of government restricting access; professionals are unable to research the impact of detention on detained children and young people.

Detained children and young people are therefore 'hidden': they do not have a voice, do not have names, and do not have visibility.

Since 1999, there have been more than five thousand asylum seeking children locked up in Australia's immigration detention centers (HREOC, 2004:61). In November 2001 a total of 521 children under the age of 18 were in immigration detention. Fifty three were unaccompanied minors. Ninety four percent of children and families were in isolated centers, such as Woomera, rather than in urban immigration detention centres. They predominantly come from Afghanistan, Iran and Iraq and have arrived on Australian shores by boat (Mares, Newman, Dudley & Gale, 2002a).

Concern for asylum seekers, and their children in particular, has been growing among legal, mental health, welfare and human rights workers (Becker & Silove, 1993).

As access to detention centres is limited and research suppressed, information on the impact of detention on children and young people in Australia to date takes the form of reports by those professionals who have visited or worked at the centres and the testimonies they have gathered from children, young people and their families. These reveal significant social/psychological disturbances.

This chapter intersperses the testimonies of some of the young detainees and their families whom we met during a series of visits to detention centres, including Woomera, over the period of time 2001–02, with the existing literature on the mental health of asylum seekers. It also explores the impact on children of exposure to violence and trauma and the developmental impact of parental depression and despair (Mares, Newman, Dudley & Gale, 2002a). The testimonies were gathered and interviews done at the request of refugee lawyers to assist in psychosocial assessments of children, young people and their families.

The circumstances described below are not unique to these children and families. We believe they are representative of the experience of all children and families in immigration detention in Australia.

Their 'truths' contradict official discourse.

Detention and Child Development

Testimony: Camilla gave birth to her second child in isolation, in a hospital several hours drive from the detention centre: she was not allowed to have culturally appropriate supports. No interpreters were present, nor was her husband. The birth occurred after four weeks enforced stay in bed, in the hospital, under guard, away from her husband and toddler. The baby was born by caesarian section before, Camilla says, she experienced any contractions. Camilla says she did not understand or consent to the surgery. It appears she was not informed of the reason for her enforced bed rest or hospitalisation in spite of this being contrary to normal obstetric practices. Immediately after the birth her baby was taken from her and not returned for several days. She was unable to breastfeed when he was returned and was given no help with establishing breastfeeding. This interruption of mother/infant contact has impacted on their attachment. Camilla was taken back to the camp one week after delivery; she was given no follow up, apart from occasional visits to the ACM nurse, who gave her paracetamol. Her wound continued to weep for 6 weeks and many months later remains painful. She says she feels violated and disenfranchised. The effect of the five week separation on her two year old toddler was significant; his behaviour deteriorated during and after his separation from her. His sense of secure attachment has been unable to be restored. Camilla's relationship with the father of her children is also under stress. It is now five months after the birth and Camilla still interacts with her baby in a mechanical way. The baby, at a developmental stage when most babies interact socially at every opportunity, looks profoundly sad, has no eye contact and shows delay in social development and vocalisation (Mares, et al., 2002a). Such an outcome, of young children showing problems in their capacity to relate to others, is to be expected, since, as Rogalla notes, children born of detained parents are incarcerated from the moment of their birth in an environment that doesn't meet their developmental needs (2002).

Children's opportunities for safe play and exploration are severely curtailed in detention. Woomera, in particular, is a hot, dusty place, unrelieved by trees or grass. A few small green areas are around the Australian Correctional Management (ACM) and Department of Immigration, Migration and Indigenous Affairs (DIMIA) offices but this area is not accessible to detainees. There is no grass for young children to learn to crawl or walk on. A few children stand out in the open, hanging onto the fence staring through the wire or kicking stones or moving wheelie bins from one place to another; many lie on their beds all day. There is nothing to do. Children in detention receive little if any education. TV footage shown early in 2002 on Australian television showed children at Woomera going to primary school, but high school age children told us that there was no educational program for nine months up to the date we arrived (Monday 7th January). None of the education services at any of the Australian detention centres would be considered acceptable if given to other children in Australia (PAHASC, 2002:23).

The dehumanising experience of being identified with their parents, by number not name, is commonplace for young detainees. Children may not have culturally appropriate clothes or even clothes that fit them. When she asked for clothes that would fit herself and her children Camilla was told to 'make them out of the curtains'. This would leave her family with no privacy, however, as windows in the camp have no screens and in a place where temperatures reach up to 50 degrees celsius, hot sun burns through unprotected windows.

In sum, detention centres are not an appropriate environment for developing children: indefinite detention erodes their identity, their culture and their humanity.

Appropriate facilities for women and children are lacking. Teenage girls tell us of needing to be escorted by parents to the toilet blocks because of harassment by other detainees. Moreover, toilets have been blood stained and filthy (Dr Annie Sparrow, former doctor at Woomera detention centre reported that 'unhygienic toilets are commonly the cause of the spread of disease within the centre' PAHASC, 2002:26). Toilet blocks have been without toilet paper or showerheads that work. 'The situation here is turning us all into savages', one father says, 'whatever laws we had in our own place are breaking down here where we are treated as less than human'.

The impact of processes of dehumanisation in detention recall something of von Neurath's experience when Jews from a nearby concentration camp were sent on work detail to her property, in Nazi Germany. Shocked at how thin they were, she describes boiling a kettle of potatoes to give them food, having them rush the kettle, spilling the potatoes, fighting for the now dirty potatoes. 'What kind of people are these?' she asked 'they are no longer human beings'. The guard replied that they were Jews, subhuman. Suddenly, said von Neurath's daughter, they heard a low soft voice behind them speaking excellent German 'It's you who've made us into animals ...' These words, von Neurath said, gave her an understanding that these were people and they needed help (Fogelman, 1994:41).

The riots at detention centres, which have received so much negative publicity, as well as lipsewing and the self-harm behaviour of young people, may be better understood if viewed as a reflection of processes of dehumanisation rather than as acts of 'manipulation' or 'blackmail' (Canberra Times Online, 16/06/02).

Negative experiences in childhood impair emotional development causing suffering in later life. The way we are treated as small children, Alice Miller observes, is the way we treat ourselves the rest of our life. Children learn respect from being respected and children who are cared for learn to care. Children who are accepted cannot learn intolerance. In an environment of respect, care and acceptance the values they develop can be nothing other than humane (Miller, 1985:97). Infants and young children like Camilla's baby, are particularly vulnerable to the effects of stress and sensitive to the emotional state of the adults around them. These children are spending a crucial formative period in abnormal environments (Newman, 2001).

Trauma in the first three years produces adverse effects on brain development (Debellis, 2001). Early trauma has a key impact on neurobiological and psychological development. It has been linked to ongoing vulnerability to stress and a range of mental health problems such as anxiety and depression. The trauma of detention and the effects on young children of parental problems such as severe depression and post traumatic stress disorder are likely to have very serious consequences (Newman, 2001; Debellis, 2001; PAHASC, 2002:14).

Children (Re)traumatized in Detention

Prior to their arrival in Australia asylum seeking children have had multiple experiences of loss and usually trauma in their countries of origin. Living in a detention centre environment exposes children and young people to violence resulting in re traumatisation as well as unrelieved contact with distressed, angry, hopeless and frequently suicidal adults. Children at these centres are terrified witnesses of suicide attempts and riots in which officers wear full riot gear and people get injured and beaten (PAHASC, 2002:6972). Their distraught parents cannot protect them.

> Testimony: During recent protests at their detention centre, three-yearold Rias and his two older sisters saw officers, come in antiriot uniforms and beat people with batons. Rias saw people toppled by the water cannon, lying motionless on the ground. Since the fires and riots the three year old has been eating poorly, clingy, unable to play, crying at night, and bedwetting.

At Woomera we see many mattresses outside in the sun, lying against the barbed wire fences. Dr Annie Sparrow observed that at Woomera bedwetting is a common problem among child detainees (PAHASC, 2002:18). We are told that many of the children, even up to the age of 12, have regressed in the detention environment and are incontinent day and night.

Nine year old Meera and her family have been in Woomera detention centre for 12 months now. She wets the bed every night. She has intrusive memories of an incident of persecution in her homeland. Her trauma is compounded by her experience of Woomera detention centre. For these past 12 months she has had daily severe headaches and frequent vomiting associated with re-traumatisation. Like other children we meet, Meera is preoccupied with living in a cage. She spontaneously draws a picture of a bird in a cage. The door and lock on the cage are heavy. The bird is on a perch but it is suspended in mid air. The bird's eyes are heavy as are its tears. When asked about the drawing, she says 'I am the bird'. She has problems sleeping: grinding her teeth at night and suffering from recurrent, distressing nightmares. She is hyper-vigilant and at night a parent has to stay near her before she can sleep.

Arnold Zable, writing in The Age (12 October) of his visit to Maribyrnong detention centre, observed that '[T]he children display the classic symptoms of trauma resulting from incarceration. These include bed-wetting, sudden bouts of anger and periods of withdrawal and depression. Some wake up screaming from nightmares' (Raynor, 2001).

Children and young people as part of their daily lives fear the guards as perpetrators of violence. Meera does not understand why she is locked up; she asks constantly why she is in prison. She protests to her father that he promised he would 'bring the family somewhere where they could be protected'. She says, 'The shadows of the guards in the Woomera camp are like the soldiers in X — (her country of origin)'. Meera's traumatic state worsened after the recent riots. Her family had no participation in the riots, however, terrified of the fire she ran, screaming in distress, around the camp trying to run away from the fire and hide.

Stimuli do not have to replicate exactly the pre existing triggers to cause flashbacks and intrusive phenomena according to Becker and Silove (1993). Barbed wire surrounding detention centres, people in uniforms, prison like conditions, being shadowed by guards, water cannons at the gates, not having access outside and many other conditions can constitute stressors that reactivate and compound pre-existing reactions (Becker & Silove, 1993).

During protests and riots these stressors become extreme. Zarah and Farina, two girls of 15 and 13, were at the other end of their centre during recent riots. They said they saw the smoke and fire and thought their room was on fire. They panicked. It was 'like the war, people were running everywhere, their faces were covered, it was dark, everyone was shouting and screaming'. In this family their father and both Zarah and Farina are depressed and suicidal.

Independently verified accounts suggest that when particular children or their families protest they are punished by coercive disciplinary strategies, for example, reports of children placed in solitary confinement, in the case of some young people, for extended periods (Dudley, 2002). Children also have, at times, become negotiating pawns in attempts to contain protests within detention centres. For example, on a number of occasions, the authorities have separated children from their parents as a measure to pressure adults to cease their hunger strikes (Sultan & O'Sullivan, 2001:595). Detention centre staff sometimes treat children and their parents in threatening, insulting and humiliating ways: we were given accounts of children being called 'little terrorists', 'towel heads' or 'queue jumpers' by some ACM staff. Such behaviours by custodial staff as well as their defensive management of children and young people can, as noted above, have a long term impact on the way the children see themselves as adults and in their relationships with other people.

Detention Undermines Parenting

His mother tells us that three year old Rias, with no other activities to engage in, used to take interest in watching the trucks and mechanical equipment around the compound. This was by far his favourite and almost only activity but since the fire engines and the water cannons had come, he does not look at the trucks and mechanical equipment any more, instead he is now always very afraid of them. 'I try to tell him it's OK now' his mother says, 'but how do I know that is true? They can come again, it can happen again at any time.' Rias' mother is unable to protect her child from exposure to violence or brutality of guards or the overwhelming experience of riots and fires. Nor can she or other parents know when these things will occur again — in an hour or not for several months.

'Please take our child and find a place for him away from here' a mother begs for her two year old. 'He will change into a savage not a human. Please find a family to care for him until we can look after him again. He doesn't trust in us anymore. He can't play, he won't eat and he doesn't sleep'. The two year old boy throws any toys offered him away; he spits at people and tries to eat bits of foam that lay on the floor. His parents say, 'You see his behaviour? It is because we are sad and weeping all the time. He has lost his trust in us'. 'We came here hoping to be free but this is worse. There is a big possibility that I kill myself here' his father says, 'I am a dead man, every day I am dying slowly. I have brought my family to hell'. Immigration detention profoundly undermines parenting. Parents have no control over the environment and are frequently too distressed themselves to be able to comfort their children. It is these circumstances, where children's distress is essentially unmediated, which are so damaging. Not uncommonly, even very young children comfort and try to parent their own parents.

One two and a half year old little girl, since being in detention, has taken up smoking and spending time with boys as comfort seeking behaviour. Her mother, profoundly depressed, cannot provide comfort for her daughter. Instead a role reversal has taken place and the little girl, with the verbal age of a five year old, is often seen sitting beside her mother saying, 'don't cry I'll look after you' (Mares, Newman, Dudley & Gale, 2002b).

Recent research finds that sequential, recurrent trauma is much more likely than oneoff trauma to lead to long term emotional difficulties and problems in coping (Becker & Silove, 1993). These difficulties are exacerbated when people suffer a series of traumatic incidents, especially related to persecution and confinement, do not have an environment to recover and the experience mimics or replicates earlier trauma. If people fleeing from persecution hoping for relief are then faced with an enormous alien trauma their emotional difficulties are exponentially compounded. In such cases, Becker and Silove argue, detention is a highly important factor. 'Eight years of witnessing war and blood in my country are better than one year in this camp' Zarah and Farina's father told us.

Suicide and Self-harm in Detention

Testimony: Zarah and Farina witnessed their father make a significant suicide attempt after their application for refugee status was refused after over seven months waiting. After this he reportedly spent several days in what he said was isolation in a police cell. He did not seem to have been offered psychiatric assessment or help. He said 'even if we get our freedom, we will be mad people by then'. At sensitive and crucial stages in their lives young people like Zarah and Farina are traumatised in a context where their parents are not able to offer comfort and protection, but because of their own intense hopelessness and depression may at times be adding to their children's trauma and anxiety. Children and young people are profoundly concerned about threats to their caregivers. For children threats to their caregiver can be even more disturbing than direct threats to themselves (Mares, Newman, Dudley & Gale, 2002b). Both Zarah and Farina are frequently tearful and often cry at night. The younger, Farina, reported being fearful of sleep, lying awake until 4 am, having nightmares, then unable to wake in the mornings. She repeatedly dreamed and visualised scenes of her father being covered in blood. Both girls said they have repeated thoughts of suicide.

Incarceration places vulnerable (youth) populations, such as (Aboriginal) youth in custody and prisoners, at high risk of selfharm (Dudley, 2002). Detainee children and young people have committed no crime, nor are they illegal yet, as one commentator describes, they are in the position of being detained indefinitely without trial (William Maley, personal communication, August 2002).

Known rates of self-harm in detention, which are likely to be underestimates, are vastly in excess of estimated community rates of self-harm (CCJDP, 2002; Dudley, 2002). Even pre-school and primary school age children, who, in the broader community, almost never make suicide attempts, are involved. Serious methods such as hanging, throat-slashing, deep wrist cutting and drinking shampoo are used.

Nine year old Meera has seen people in the compound cutting themselves, hanging themselves or taking overdoses. She expresses the feeling that she 'should cut herself too, like that man' (speaking of another detainee she had seen slashing his wrists). Meera has since made serious suicide attempts including cutting herself, drinking shampoo and hanging herself with a sheet.

Elevated rates of self-harm reflect the continuum of negligence that is immigration detention. The policies pursued by DIMIA are directly opposed to official suicide prevention policies of the Commonwealth Government. Given the former Immigration Minister's unwillingness to consult with his Government's advisers in suicide prevention, these policies appear to be kept as far apart as possible (Dudley, 2002).

> Testimony: Abu, 17 and Hassan, 15, are brothers and current detainees with their parents and younger two sisters. Abu experiences suicidal thoughts, hopelessness, head banging, recurring nightmares of barbed wire fences. 'After this fence, there's no life, it's like hell'. When we first meet him, he is sad, agitated and preoccupied and gazes into the distance. Hassan has made a series of serious suicide attempts (by electrocution, hunger strike, hanging attempt narrowly averted, selfcutting). He says he hopes to 'sleep, wake up and find freedom'.

The family have been in various detention centres for 21 months. When both brothers escaped in a riot two years ago, police returned them, allegedly beating and kicking them. Abu describes being handcuffed and left in a poorly lit small room for a week, with no toilet or washing facilities, only a thin blanket and freezing air-conditioning (which, he reports, guards refused to turn off). He witnessed a prolonged beating in which he thought the victim might be killed. Further hunger strikes and lip-sewing occurred over the progress of their visa applications: Abu, Hassan and their father were separated from the rest of the family.

In August 2000, Abu, Hassan, their father and three other adolescent asylum seekers were handcuffed and taken by staff in full riot gear to maximum security. The rest of the detainees started a hunger strike and they were released. Later the same month, 2025 riot staff allegedly burst in on the family at 5 am, and handcuffed the older members. Different family members were put in separate cells (one for their mother and two youngest children, one for father and Hassan, and one each for Abu and an older brother). The family spent 15 days in cell block. There were no working showers, no toilet facilities in cells. The younger children and mother reported that they had to use a plastic bag, which they found in the cell. Their mother found this unhygienic and humiliating, she went on a hunger strike for two days before guards would allow them to use the toilet. The younger children remain highly distressed by the effect of forcible separations from their parents and sometimes even their older brothers (leaving them alone in detention to care for themselves) and by many acts of witnessed violence.

In March 2001, Hassan took rope from washing line and found a place under stairs where he could hang himself while his parents were at dinner. He was found by chance by another detainee. After treatment in a psychiatric hospital, recommendations that he be released from detention were ignored and he was returned to detention. More recently, in a different detention centre, he made another attempt, was treated by another hospital and again was returned to detention. He remains a significant suicide risk. Recommendations for his release from detention continue to be ignored.

Many factors account for children and young people's mental health problems, suicidal behaviour and violence in detention centres. Principal among these, however, is the extremity of the detention environment. The indeterminacy of detention and the time consuming, legalistic, adversarial nature of the refugee determination process make detention a formidable endurance test (PAHASC, 2002:218). Clinical reports, narratives by detainees and accounts of other observers confirm that children, like adults, suffer from depression, anxiety and posttraumatic stress disorder (PTSD) and from disrupted attachments and development. This testimony also suggests that these disturbances are greatly augmented by detention. There is a serious risk in the present situation that someone will die. Access to means of selfharm in detention is restricted and suicidal detainees are closely watched, however, without change in their circumstances, this may have the effect of increasing suicidality. For true resolution, suicidal and selfharming people require a humane and empathic response, a 'circle of safety'. This requires their immediate environmental stresses to be relieved, especially if these are severe or extreme. There is no doubt that the detention environment is extreme.

Understanding self-harm among detained asylum seeking young people presents unique challenges. Detainees' lip sewing is a symbol of their being silenced. Lip sewing is also an action against perceived injustice. This may take on alarming proportions, such as children imitating self-harm by adults or older siblings. In this tragedy, asylum seekers' motivations include both despair and protest. The wish to die and the wish to get someone to take notice or to change one's circumstances are closely related. Protest, despair and children's imitation of self-harming acts are important motivations for selfharm in detention centres. However, the former Minister only really sees protest as significant: he defines self-harm as 'manipulation' or 'blackmail' (Canberra Times Online, 16/06/02). This continues the reproduction of outdated yet persistent attitudes to self-harm among the Australian public, where suicide and self-harm are often poorly understood. The national suicide prevention strategy, funded by the Commonwealth government, has been trying to address such attitudinal problems, emphasizing the importance of taking people attempting suicide and engaging in self-harm seriously rather than regarding them as behaving badly or simply manipulative (Dudley, 2002). This again illustrates the disjunction between the official policies on suicide and self-harm and the political management of 'truth'.

These understandings of peoples' detained lives are not new. We know from medical and sociological literature that detention re-traumatises and causes further harm to those detained. Given the findings of increased trauma due to effects of detention, the incarceration of children is strongly counter indicated from a psycho-medical perspective. A vast literature demonstrates the impact on children of exposure to trauma and violence (Pynoos & Nader, 1989; Pynoos & Eth, 1985; Kinzie, Sack, Angell & Clarke, 1989; Pfefferbaum, 1997), the impact of parental mental illness on social and emotional development [particularly in the context of other environmental stressors] (Golpert, Webster & Seeman, 1996), and the long term developmental and health consequences of this exposure (Blank, 1993; Debellis, 2001).

Literature

Refugee children and adolescents have diverse experiences; many however, have witnessed or experienced the death or murder of loved ones. Those who seek asylum are uprooted from their family, friends, location, culture and everything that is familiar to them: multiple losses are the centre of their experiences (Berman, 2001:1, 2). Yet, as ex-Woomera nurse Barbara Rogalla observes, instead of providing an environment in which healing can occur, we perpetuate the trauma through indefinite detention (Rogalla, 2002).

Studying the mental health and social adjustment of young refugee children three and a half years after their arrival in Sweden, Almqvist and Brodberg (1999) found that their adaptation is the result of complex processes which involve several interacting risk and protective factors. Startlingly their findings were that for many refugee children, their 'current life circumstances in receiving host countries' are of 'equal or greater importance than previous exposure to organised violence' (Almqvist & Brodberg, 1999:1).

There are few studies of children in detention, however, there are now many studies which document the problems experienced by adult refugees and asylum seekers (Silove, Steel & Watters, 2000). Detained Tamil asylum seekers, for example, exhibit higher levels of depression and PTSD than compatriots living in the community. Similarly, in examining factors which contribute to adaptive functioning once people were given asylum in the United States, Rumbaut found that length of stay in detention camps overseas evidenced high psychological distress scores and poorer capacity to adapt to the new environment. Psychological distress, he reiterated, was consistently linked to conditions of powerlessness and alienation unbuffered by networks of socio-emotional support (Rumbaut quoted in Becker & Silove, 1993).

Rumbaut concluded that the length of stay in refugee camps or detention centres has a significant effect on the psychological functioning of the detainees or refugees and that well being deteriorates over time irrespective of other factors (Becker & Silove, 1993).

Despite this information the Government has chosen to construct the situation of asylum seekers as one of 'illegals' who should be made an example of. The current government have presented a very different picture of the plight of asylum seekers and privileged one version of events over many other interpretations.

The Politics of 'Truth'

Near the end of 2000, the children in detention issue became publicly visible, through the case of Shayan Badraie. Six year old Shayan had witnessed another detainee attempt suicide. After this he became mute and stopped eating. A public debate followed. Assessing mental health professionals argued strongly that Shayan was traumatised by his experience in Australian detention centres and that he should be removed from detention and not returned (Four Corners, 13/08/01). The then Minister, however, dismissed these assessments and publicly attributed Shayan's state to his family situation. In response, assessing professionals said that they did not consider his family structure to be a factor (7.30 Report, 14/08/01). In other words, the Minister, who says he based his claims on medical advice he received, applied a medical diagnosis of individual 'pathology'. Those who are so labeled are silenced through their 'pathologisation'.

Although medicine and the law maintain relative autonomy in democracies, they may, as Scraton notes, be 'harnessed to the material interests of the state'. In their application they often endorse 'social exclusion' rather than 'effectively challenging its ... basis'. Scraton observes that as professions law and medicine are connected to maintaining and reproducing established orders (2002:4,5).

In detention Zarah and Farina have been treated as 'individuals who have problems' rather than their detention environment seen as problematic. Both teenagers were treated by an ACM psychologist, but both said they had not found this helpful. The psychologist had offered sleeping tablets and tranquilisers but 'they just make us sleep all day'. Both these teenagers have been subdued through 'pathologisation'. Both remain profoundly depressed and suicidal. Acting in this capacity ACM psychologists contribute to the 'official discourse', the institutional processes and professional interventions which become expressions of power 'legitimating' the state's 'self serving versions of 'truth'' (Scraton, 2002:4).

DIMIA's recent submission to the Human Rights and Equal Opportunity Commission enquiry concerning children in detention illustrates the 'official discourse' very well. Rather than acknowledging the impact of detention it stated of children in detention, 'children who present with emotional issues may have parents who also have pre-existing predispositions toward depression and/or poor coping skills' (Taylor, 2002).

Negative imagery and established ideologies, Scraton and Chadwick observe, successfully deflect responsibility away from the state (1987:7). Self-harm, threats of suicide and lip sewing have been defined by the Minister for Immigration as manipulative as well as 'inappropriate behaviour', 'intimidating us with our own decency', and 'blackmail' (Canberra Times Online, 16/06/02). Reports of suicides are minimised. A number of health professionals who work with refugees have commented that Minister Ruddock is 'attributing malevolence and manipulation by the detainees', to 'demean and devalue the cry for assistance that children are making' (Metherell, 2002). The Government and DIMIA's behaviour is a clear example of the political management of identity which involves 'a process of categorisation' suggesting that the 'alien', the 'dangerous' or the 'violent' contribute to their own critical situation 'either by their pathological condition or personal choice' (Scraton & Chadwick, 1987:7).

Any alternative accounts of children and young people in mandatory detention are disqualified or dismissed by the government. The Human Right's Commissioner, Sev Ozdowski, after conducting an investigation at Woomera detention centre, stated that conditions at the Woomera centre placed Australia in breach of its obligation under the UN Convention on the Rights of the Child. The Minister summarily dismissed the Commissioner's findings (AAP, 07/02/02). Not dissimilarly, DIMIA has ignored advice from some child protection authorities refusing to release from detention centres some at-risk children (Lateline, 01/05/02). DIMIA has made many statements in an effort to discredit its critics: for example, the Minister's statement attempting to discredit the Four Corners program concerning the case of Shayan Bedraie (Ruddock, 16/08/01).

One approach to criticism used by the Minister's has been to 'blame the critic' as the cause of the problems. For example, in response to criticism from the recent visiting UN Detention Enquiry Delegation, DIMIA condemned the UN Delegation itself: too many visits, DIMIA said, upset detainees (AAP, 2002). The Minister went on to make the claim that detention centres were fine for children (Taylor, 2002).

The voices of detainees are silenced through government 'labeling' and 'pathologising', and alternative accounts by critics are dismissed or nullified. The Government and DIMIA cast their critics aside 'through denials and rationalizations, their own actions neutralized and their condemners condemned' (Scraton, 2002:15, 16; Cohen, 2001:97).

'Truth', as Foucault argues, 'is produced and sustained within the dominant, structural relations of power' (Foucault, 1980:131). As 'voices from behind the razor wire', the testimonies given here protest the Government's construction of 'truth'.

Turning his head away from the wire and the desert, looking at us with large puzzled eyes, three year old Rias asks 'Why aren't there any flowers in Australia?'

REFERENCES

ABC (2002), 'Government comes under fire for detention centre children', Lateline, 1 May 2002.

ABC (2001), 'The Inside Story' Reported by Debbie Whitmont, Four Corners, 13 Aug 2001.

ABC (2001), 'Four Corners program gives insight into plight of detainees' Reported by Debbie Whitmont, 7.30 Report, 14 Aug 2001.

Australian Associated Press (2002), 7 February.

Australian Associated Press (2002), 'Ruddock says visitors encourage detainee self harm', Sydney Morning Herald, 6 June 2002.
    http://www.smh.com.au/articles/2002/06/06/102298 2742418.html.

Almqvist, K. & Brodberg, A. (1999), 'Mental health and social adjustment in young refugee children 3 1/2 years after their arrival in Sweden', Journal of the American Academy of Child and Adolescent Psychiatry, ' 38 (6), June, 723–730.

Banham, C. (2002), 'Woomera conditions likened to Nazi days', Sydney Morning Herald, 20 Sept 2002, p. 3.

Becker, R. & Silove, D. (1993), 'The Psychological and Psychosocial Effects of Prolonged Detention' (pp.81-90) in M. Crock (Ed.), Protection or Punishment: the Detention of Asylum Seekers in Australia. Sydney: The Federation Press.

Berman, H. (2001), 'Children and war: Current Understandings and Future Directions', Public Health Nursing, 18(4), July/August, 243252.

Blank, A. (1993), 'The longitudinal course of posttraumatic stress disorder' (pp. 322), in J. Davidson and E. Foa (Eds.), Post Traumatic Stress Disorder: DSM iv and Beyond. Washington DC: American Psychiatric Press.

Canberra Times Online (2002), Canberra.yourguide.com.au, 16th June 2002.

CCJDP (Catholic Commission for Justice Development and Peace), (2002), Damaging Kids: Children in Department of Immigration and Multicultural and Indigenous Affairs ', Immigration Detention Centres, Occasional Paper No. 12, May.

Cohen, S. (2001), States of Denial: Knowing About Atrocities and Suffering, Cambridge: Polity Press.

Debellis, M. (2001), 'Developmental traumatology: The psychobiological development of maltreated children', Development and Psychopathology, 13, 5 3 95 6 4.

Dudley, M. (2002), 'Two Australian National Policies on SelfInjury and Suicide', Section of Social and Cultural Psychiatry of the Royal Australian and NZ College of Psychiatrists in association with the Public Health Association of Australia and the Australian Association of Social Workers, Triennial Conference, Cairns, 1214 September.

Fogelman, E. (1994), *Conscience and Courage: Rescuers of Jews during the Holocaust*. New York: Doubleday.

Foucault, M. (1980), *Power/Knowledge: Selected Interviews and Other Writings 1972-1977*, C. Gordon (Ed.). Brighton: Harvester Wheatsheaf.

Golpert, M., Webster, T. & Seeman, M. (1996), *Parental Psychiatric Disorder: Distressed parents and their children*. Cambridge: Cambridge University Press.

HREOC (Human Rights and Equal Opportunity Commission), (2004), 'A last resort' the Report of the National Inquiry into Children in Immigration Detention. Human Rights and Equal Opportunity Commisssion: Sydney.

Kinzie, J., Sack, W., Angell, R. & Clarke, G. (1989), 'A three year follow up of Cambodian young people traumatized as children', *Journal of the American Academy of Child and Adolescent Psychiatry*, 28, 501 504.

Mares, S., Newman, L., Dudley, M. & Gale, F. (2002a), 'Seeking refuge, losing hope: parents and children in immigration detention', *Australasian Psychiatry*, 10 (2), 91-97.

Mares, S., Newman, L., Dudley, M. & Gale, F. (2002b), 'The Wire and Us Behind It', Section of Social and Cultural Psychiatry of the Royal Australian and NZ College of Psychiatrists in association with the Public Health Association of Australia and the Australian Association of Social Workers, Triennial Conference, Cairns, 1214 September.

Metherell, M. (2002), 'Copycat risk after threats of suicide', *Sydney Morning Herald*, 30 Jan 2002, p. 2.

Miller, A. (1985), *Though Shalt Not be Aware: Society's Betrayal of the Child*. London: Pluto Press.

Newman, L. (2001), 'The plight of babies born behind barbed wire', *Sydney Morning Herald*, 24 Dec 2001, p. 12.

PAHASC (Professional Alliance for the Health of Asylum Seekers and their Children), (2002), Inquiry into Children in Immigration Detention, Submission to the Human Rights and Equal Opportunity Commission, May, 2002.

Pfefferbaum, B. (1997), 'Post traumatic stress disorder in children: A review of the past 10 years', *Journal of the American Academy of Child and Adolescent Psychiatry*, 36,1503–1511.

Pynoos, R. & Eth, S. (1985), 'Witnessing acts of personal violence' (pp. 1743) in S. Eth & R. Pynoos (Eds.), *Post Traumatic Stress in Children. Washington DC*: American Psychiatric Press.

Pynoos, R. & Nader K. (1989), 'Children's memory and proximity to violence', *Journal of the American Academy of Child and Adolescent Psychiatry*, 28, 501504.

Raynor, M. (2001), *Political Pinballs: The Plight of Child Refugees in Australia*, Walter Murdoch Lecture, 31 Oct 2001.

Rogalla, B. (2002), 'Children In Detention', Sydney's Child, February.

Ruddock, P. (2001), 'Rebuttal of Four Corners Program', M P S 118/2001, 16 Aug 2001.

Scraton, P. (2002), 'Lost Lives, Hidden Voices: 'Truth' and Controversial Deaths', Race and Class, JulySeptember, 44,107119.

Scraton, P. & Chadwick, K. (1987), 'Speaking Ill of the Dead': Institutionalised Responses to Deaths in Custody', in P. Scraton (Ed.), *Law, Order and the Authoritarian State*. Milton Keynes: Open University Press.

Silove, D., Steel, Z. & Watters, C. (2000), 'Policies of deterrence and the mental health of asylum seekers', *Journal of the American Medical Association*, 284 (5), 604611.

Sultan, A. & O'Sullivan, K. (2001), 'Psychological disturbances in asylum seekers held in longterm detention: a participant observer account', *Medical Journal of Australia*, 175, 593596.

Taylor, K. (2002), 'Government defends treatment of children in detention', *The Age*, 30 May 2002, http://www.theage.com.au/articles/2002/05/29/1022 569792632.html.

ACKNOWLEDGEMENTS

We thank Sarah Mares, Louise Newman, Phil Scraton and Karen Wilcox. We also thank detainees, who asked us to tell people 'on the other side of the wire' about their experiences.

CHAPTER FIVE
CHILDREN'S RIGHTS HUMAN RIGHTS

CHRIS SIDOTI

Introduction

Australian law, policy and practice in relation to asylum seekers and refugees, as they are in 2002, violate the human rights commitments made over the past 50 years by successive Australian Governments under a number of international treaties. The violations are not trivial or few. They are many, flagrant and gross. They are the direct and inevitable result of the bipartisan policies of successive governments since 1989, both Coalition and Labor, under three Prime Ministers. Only the Australian Democrats, the Greens, independents Brian Harradine and Peter Andren and a handful of members from the major parties have struggled against the odds to prevent these violations and so far they have not been successful. While responsibility falls on both major parties, the government, under Prime Minister Howard and Immigration Minister Ruddock, has taken us to the murkiest, nastiest depths in which we now stand accused and convicted of gross violations of the fundamental human rights of some of the most vulnerable people within Australia's jurisdiction.

The Scope of the Violations

The human rights violations arise under almost all the major human rights treaties.

First is the Convention Relating to the Status of Refugees 1951 (the Refugees Convention) itself. Article 31 of the Convention prohibits the imposition of penalties on refugees on account of their illegal entry or presence. In particular, in paragraph 2, it provides: 'The Contracting States shall not apply to the movements of such refugees, restrictions other than those which are necessary'.

In November 2001, the United Nations High Commissioner for Refugees convened a roundtable of 30 international experts to consider these provisions of the Convention. Robert Illingworth and I were among those participants. The roundtable adopted a consensus statement that reflected the views of the majority of experts present of the requirements of international law.

In the consensus statement the international experts said that the protections of Article 31 applied to both those recognised as refugees and to those still seeking asylum. They applied not only to those entering a country directly from a country of persecution but also to those 'who have briefly transited other countries or who are unable to find effective protection in the first country or countries to which they flee'. Any detention of refugees and asylum seekers, to be lawful, had to be based on an assessment of the need to detain a particular individual and be subject to judicial review. They said that detention was never justifiable for the purposes of deterrence. The experts said:

> The detention of refugees and asylum seekers is an exceptional measure and should only be applied in the individual case, where it has been determined by the appropriate authority to be necessary in light of the circumstances of the case and on the basis of criteria established by law in line with international refugee and human rights law. As such, it should not be applied unlawfully and arbitrarily and only where it is necessary for the reasons outlined in ExCom Conclusion no. 44, in particular for the protection of national security and public order (e.g. risk of absconding). National law and practice should take full account of the international obligations accepted by States, including through regional and universal human rights treaties.
>
> Initial periods of administrative detention for the purposes of identifying refugees and asylum seekers and of establishing the elements for their claim to asylum should be minimised. In particular, detention should not be extended for the purposes of punishment, or maintained where asylum procedures are protracted.

The concluding statement also referred to the situation of families and children:

> Families and children, in particular, should be treated in accordance with international standards and children under eighteen ought never to be detained. Families should in principle not be detained; where this is the case, they should not be separated.

The statement accepted that some restriction may be required for those not in detention but said that any restriction should be the minimum necessary on an individually assessed basis. It stated strongly the right to have effective judicial review of detention and the right to access legal advice and assistance and to be advised of that right:

> In terms of procedural safeguards, at a minimum, there should be a right to review the legality and the necessity of detention before an independent court or tribunal, in accordance with the rule of law and the principles of due process. Refugees and asylumseekers should be advised of their legal rights, have access to counsel and to national courts and tribunals and be enabled to contact the Office of UNHCR (United Nations Human Rights Commissioner).

Australian law and practice do not accord with this statement of the international legal situation. Asylum seekers who come as unlawful non-citizens, that is, as boat people, are subjected to a regime of indefinite mandatory detention. There is no individual assessment of the need to detain or of the minimum level of restriction required. Everyone is detained, including families and children, even unaccompanied minors. The period in detention has extended up to five and a half years. There is no possibility of effective judicial review of the detention or of the need to detain. A detainee is not even told what rights he or she has under Australian and international law. There is a right to legal advice and representation but no entitlement under Australian law to be told that right — and government directions to public servants and detention centre staff are that detainees are not to be told. Although in the past government ministers and immigration officials were careful to avoid saying that these policies were for the purpose of deterrence, all pretence has been abandoned over the last year and defence of the policy is now based principally on 'sending a message' to other wouldbe asylum seekers.

The views expressed by the international experts in this UNHCR roundtable were firmly based not only on the provisions of Refugees Convention and also on the provisions of other international human rights treaties. The detention regime imposed by Australian law and the practice of detention violate many of these other provisions, including:

- article 9 of the International Covenant on Civil and Political Rights and article 37 of the Convention on the Rights of the Child, which prohibit arbitrary detention;
- article 37 of the Convention on the Rights of the Child, which prohibits detention of children except as a last resort and for the shortest appropriate period of time;
- article 9 of the International Covenant on Civil and Political Rights and article 37 of the Convention on the Rights of the

Child, which recognise a right to take legal proceedings to challenge detention;

- article 2 of the International Covenant on Civil and Political Rights and article 2 of the International Covenant on Economic, Social and Cultural Rights, which prohibit all discrimination on the basis of status in the enjoyment of human rights;
- article 10 of the International Covenant on Civil and Political Rights and article 37 of the Convention on the Rights of the Child, which require that detained persons be treated with humanity and respect for human dignity;
- article 22 of the Convention on the Rights of the Child, which requires the state to provide appropriate protection and humanitarian assistance to refugee and asylum seeker children; articles 13 and 15 of the International Covenant on Economic, Social and Cultural Rights and article 28 of the Convention on the Rights of the Child, which recognise children's right to education;
- articles 12 of the International Covenant on Economic, Social and Cultural Rights and article 24 of the Convention on the Rights of the Child, which recognise children's right to the highest attainable standard of health and facilities for the treatment of mental and physical illness; and
- article 31 of the Convention on the Rights of the Child, which recognise children's right to play and recreational activities and to participate fully in cultural and artistic life.

In addition to this catalogue of clear violations there are questions whether other human rights obligations have been breached, especially in relation to:

- article 6 of the International Covenant on Civil and Political Rights, article 37 of the Convention on the Rights of the Child and the Convention Against Torture and Other Cruel, Inhuman or Degrading Treatment or Punishment, which prohibit torture and all cruel, inhuman and degrading treatment and punishment; and
- article 2 of the International Covenant on Civil and Political Rights and article 2 of the International Covenant on Economic, Social and Cultural Rights, which prohibit all discrimination on the basis of religion and race in the enjoyment of human rights

and the Convention on the Elimination of All Forms of Racial Discrimination.

These provisions relate to conditions in detention, extending the obligations in article 10 of the International Covenant on Civil and Political Rights and article 37 of the Convention on the Rights of the Child, which require that detained persons be treated with humanity and respect for human dignity. The situation in the camps in Australia, euphemistically called Immigration Reception and Processing Centres, is appalling. Between 1995 and 2000 I visited each camp at least once a year. In some cases conditions were worse than I had found in any Australian prison. And I understand that they have deteriorated badly since then. Disturbances and riots are expected and entirely predictable. There is a long and continuing history of selfharm in the camps and hunger strikes have become common place. The detainees are frustrated, alienated and fearful. They are exposed to routine violence and severe mental health episodes. The camps are particularly awful for children. The disturbances in the camps over the last year have been provoked, consciously or unconsciously, by deliberate policy and administrative decisions, like the suspension of processing of protection applications from Afghani detainees November 2001. The pattern of the past decade indicates that disturbances will continue and worsen and that lives, both of detainees and of the centre officers, will be at risk. Current policies ensure that the government and its contractors are powerless to prevent it.

The issue of family reunion requires special mention. It was the second issue discussed at the international experts roundtable convened by the UNHCR in November 2001. Again the consensus statement of the experts strongly affirmed the right of refugee families to be reunited as 'a basic human right'. It said:

- refusal to allow family reunification may be considered as an interference with the right to family life or to family unity, especially where the family has no realistic possibilities for enjoying that right elsewhere.
- requests for family reunification should be dealt with in a positive, humane and expeditious manner, with particular attention being paid to the best interests of the child … States should seek to reunite refugee families as soon as possible, and in any event, without unreasonable delay.

Again the views of the experts at the roundtable were based not only on the Refugees Convention but also on later human rights standards that assist the interpretation and application of the Convention. Australian law now distinguishes between refugees on Temporary Protection Visas (TPVs) and other refugees and immigrants, discriminating against refugees on TPVs. They are denied the opportunity to bring their spouses and children to Australia and so are condemned by the law to indefinite family separation. This violates:

- article 23 of the International Covenant on Civil and Political Rights, article 10 of the International Covenant on Economic, Social and Cultural Rights and article 18 of the Convention on the Rights of the Child, which protect the right of parents to found a family, the right of families to state care and support and the right of children to the care of their parents; and
- article 22 of the Convention on the Rights of the Child, which requires the state to provide appropriate protection and humanitarian assistance to refugee and asylum seeker children, especially in relation to family reunion.

All these violations of human rights are serious. There is not a trivial matter among them. They are all the direct result of Australian law, policy and practice and so the direct responsibility of the Australian Government and the Australian Parliament, and ultimately of us, the Australian people. Hugh Mackay, writing in the Easter weekend edition of the Sydney Morning Herald (2002) put it well:

> The names of John Howard and Philip Ruddock will be forever tarnished by their intransigence over the imprisonment of these children and the harshness of their treatment. But that won't let the rest of us off the hook. We're here. We know what's going on. Australia is doing these things and we are Australians. We're in it up to our necks (p. 28).

Human Rights and the Pacific Solution

Consideration of human rights and Australia's treatment of asylum seekers requires some comment on the socalled Pacific Solution. What the Government calls the Pacific Solution is no solution at all.

Paying another country to take the people Australia does not want does not absolve Australia from responsibility for the protection and promotion of their human rights. On the contrary, when, as here, these other countries take these people on behalf of Australia, under contract from Australia and under directions from the Australian Government, then our Government remains responsible for their enjoyment of their fundamental human rights. This is the kind of situation envisaged in Australian legislation, in the H u m a n Rights and Equal Opportunity Commission Act 1986. That Act provides that the Australian Human Rights Commission has jurisdiction in relation to 'acts and practices of the Commonwealth' which is defined as including acts and practices 'done by or on behalf of the Commonwealth'. So the Australian Government remains as liable for human rights violations in the offshore camps on Nauru and Manus Island, Papua New Guinea, as in the on-shore camps.

The Pacific Solution involves Australia in what the Government is loudest in condemning, people trafficking. It involves the apprehension and forcible transfer of people across national boundaries for profit. Desperate people are being dumped in desperately poor island states. These states are paid large bribes to accept people Australia does not want. The people dumped in this way have no guarantee of protection from persecution or from repatriation to a country where they are at risk of persecution. Indeed one of the states involved, Nauru, is not even a party to the Refugees Convention and so has no obligation under that Convention not to return asylum seekers to their country of persecution.

The socalled Pacific Solution is also troubling because it runs the risk of distorting the Australian Official Development Assistance program away from its developmental priorities (Oxfam, 2002). It encourages the use of aid as an incentive to poor states to take Australia's problem off our hands and as a penalty against those that do not.

Twelve Principles for Good Refugee Policy

We must move beyond this present sorry state. That will require a far more just approach to the treatment of asylum seekers than we have seen over the last decade. Australian refugee policy suffers a lack of principle in its basis and formulation. Present policy is reactive, piecemeal and ad hoc without any clear foundation in law or ethics, grounded in public fear and government manipulation. Before attempting to devise a new, better approach to the treatment of asylum seekers we need to articulate clear principles based on human rights and the best Australian values of decency, compassion, hospitality and fairness. We need to provide a sound moral basis for whatever laws, policies and processes we adopt. There are twelve fundamental principles that I suggest should found our policies in this area, twelve principles on which, in my view, all fair minded Australians should be able to reach agreement. They are principles that would remove from us the responsibility and the odium of being gross violators of human rights.

1. Australia is entitled to protect its borders and its territorial integrity in ways that are consistent with its domestic and international legal obligations, including its human rights obligations. It is entitled to regulate or prevent the entry of aliens into Australia provided that it does not violate its domestic and international legal obligations in doing so.

2. Australia will accord to refugees and asylum seekers all their rights and entitlements under relevant international law, including under the Refugee Convention, the International Covenant on Civil and Political Rights, the Convention on the Rights of the Child and the Torture Convention.

3. No refugee or asylum seeker will be subjected to punishment, mistreatment or other human rights violation to deter others from seeking asylum in Australia.

4. Refugees and asylum seekers who are intercepted on their way to Australia will be treated with respect for their dignity and not be subjected to physical violence or threats of physical violence.

5. Refugees and asylum seekers who are intercepted on their way to Australia will not be diverted forcibly to a third country but brought to Australia to have their claims processed in accordance with international law. Under no circumstances will a refugee or asylum seeker be diverted forcibly to a country that is not a party to the Refugee Convention or to the major human rights treaties.

6. Conditions will not be attached to Australian aid funds to require or encourage countries to intercept refugees and asylum seekers on the way to Australia or to accept refugees and asylum seekers from Australia for detention or processing. Australian aid funds will not be diverted from development projects to underpin the detention and

processing of refugees and asylum seekers in other countries.

7. Refugees and asylum seekers will not be detained arbitrarily. In particular, there will be no indefinite mandatory detention of refugees or asylum seekers. No refugee or asylum seeker should be detained beyond an initial processing period unless individually assessed, subject to judicial review, as requiring to be detained on grounds of public health, public safety or public security.

8. No refugee or asylum seeker child will be detained except as a last resort and then for the shortest possible period of time. The parents and siblings of a child, or in their absence other family members who may be with the child, will ordinarily be released with the child to provide for the child's care and wellbeing, unless their release would raise significant risks in relation to public health, public safety or public security.

9. In all decisions affecting a child the best interests of the individual child shall be a paramount consideration. Children are entitled to have their views heard and taken into account, according to their ages and maturity, in all decisions affecting them.

10. Any refugee or asylum seeker in detention is entitled to be treated humanely with respect for his or her human dignity. The standards applicable in detention will be at least no less than those to which convicted prisoners are entitled.

11. Asylum seekers who are accepted as refugees within the Refugees Convention are entitled to family reunion. Family reunion entitlements will extend at least to spouses and children and to parents and siblings who are dependent on the refugee. In the case of a refugee child, family reunion will extend without qualification to the child's parents or if the child has no parent, then to adult family members or others who might have responsibility for the care of the child.

12. Asylum seekers accepted as refugees will be accepted for permanent resettlement. They will be entitled to all the benefits to which permanent residents are entitled.

The present system of indefinite mandatory detention in inhumane conditions of virtually all asylum seekers who reach the Australian mainland and of forced international transfer and offshore detention of those who attempt to do so breaches these twelve basic principles. The principles enable us to develop an alternative approach, a better policy for refugees and asylum seekers.

An Alternative to the Present System

Developing a better approach that complies with human rights obligations is not an impossible or even a difficult task. Indeed every western country except Australia has managed to do it. The Prime Minister says he is unhappy with having to detain children, women and men seeking asylum, most of whom are refugees, and he says he does so only because he has to. The fact, however, is that he does not have to, that these detentions are the result of the deliberate policies of successive governments that have ignored or dismissed the many workable alternatives proposed over the years.

As early as 1994 a number of refugee and human rights non-government organisations and the Human Rights and Equal Opportunity Commission endorsed a Charter of Minimum Requirements for Legislation Relating to the Detention of Asylum Seekers i. The Charter provided general principles and an outline of a system to implement those principles.

In September 1996 a Detention Reform Coordinating Committee was established following the endorsement of this Charter and submitted a draft alternative detention model to the Minister for Immigration and Multicultural Affairs. Under this model, restrictions of the current type on the liberty of Protection Visa applicants are kept to a minimum, usually less than 90 days. After the initial period in closed detention most applicants would move to a more liberal regime appropriate to the individual's circumstances. Regular review of each applicant's detention status is recommended so as to improve the ability to match the restrictions imposed on an applicant's liberty to his or her circumstances (HREOC, 1998).

In 1998 the Human Rights and Equal Opportunity Commission developed that model further in a detailed proposal in its report Those who've come across the seas: detention of unauthorised arrivals (1998: 247-256). That model remains a viable, effective alternative that is fully consistent with the principles for good policy I have enunciated today.

The events of 2001 led to more work on alternative models. In June 2001 the Conference of Leaders of Religious Institutes (NSW) released a policy proposal for adjustments to Australia's asylum seeking process. Later in 2001 another nongovernment organisation, Justice for Asylum Seekers, extended this work in proposing the Transitional Processing and Reception Model.

All these models are similar. All are consistent with the twelve principles I have proposed. They constitute an acceptable and appropriate framework for a better approach to refugees and asylum seekers. The framework is clear.

First, a period of initial mandatory detention, consistent with government and opposition policy, is acceptable. International law and practice recognises that detention is permissible if required by reason of public health, public safety, public security and identification (United Nations High Commissioner for Refugees, 1986). What is not acceptable is extending mandatory detention indefinitely, denying individual assessment of the need to detain and prohibiting judicial review of detention beyond the initial period.

Significantly all those participating in the public debate about detention of asylum seekers support speedy determination of status. The present policy of indefinite detention provides no incentive whatsoever to departmental authorities to complete the process within a reasonable period of time. As a result initial processing can extend for many months, sometimes even more than a year. Limiting the period of mandatory detention will provide a powerful and effective incentive to ensure the prompt determination of applications. If departmental officials do not do their job within a reasonable period of acceptable mandatory detention, then the asylum seeker should be entitled to be considered for release, subject to whatever conditions may be determined to be necessary and prudent.

The Human Rights and Equal Opportunity Commission recommended an initial period of detention of thirty days, with two possible extensions of thirty days, making a total period of possible detention of ninety days. These proposals remain acceptable and appropriate.

Many have argued against any period of mandatory detention, no matter how brief. There are strong ethical and moral grounds for this position and so it should not be dismissed out of hand. International human rights law, however, permits a brief initial period of detention, as indicated, and the model proposed here is based upon the minimum requirements of international law. But those provisions are minimum requirements. Australia can and perhaps should look to do what is right, not merely the minimum that is required of us. Of course, the very problem with the present situation is that we are not even meeting our minimum commitments.

Second, before the end of the initial period of thirty days each asylum seeker should receive individual assessment for release. Not every asylum seeker will be released. There will be some whose continued detention is justified and reasonable and acceptable under international law. The Human Rights and Equal Opportunity Commission identified those:

- whose identity cannot be verified;
- whose application for a Protection Visa has not been lodged for processing;
- who are considered on reasonable grounds to pose a threat to national security or public order or public health or safety;
- who are assessed as very likely to abscond; or
- who refuse to undertake or fail the health screening.

The critical element is that these assessments are made on an individual, person by person, basis and not be general judgements applied to an entire group of asylum seekers or to all asylum seekers.

The Commission also listed those who should be given priority for release:

- children under 18 years of age and close relatives of a child detainee under 18 years of age;
- unaccompanied minors;
- those older than 75 years of age;
- single women;
- those requiring specialist medical attention that cannot be provided in detention; and
- those requiring specialist medical attention due to previous experience of torture or trauma and which cannot be provided appropriately in detention.

The Human Rights and Equal Opportunity Commission proposed that the initial decision on release should be made by departmental officers subject to tribunal and judicial review. Those who are not released before the end of 90 days are entitled to a statement of reasons for and judicial review of the decision to continue their detention. The model proposed by Justice for Asylum Seekers takes a different approach. It provides for release or continued detention to be determined by an assessment panel with both departmental and outside members.

Third, those who have not been properly denied release on one of the grounds set out above should be released on an appropriate bridging visa subject, where necessary, to restrictions on movement. The bridging visa may provide certain restrictions on the freedom of movement of the asylum seeker. The Human Rights and Equal Opportunity Commission proposed two types of bridging visa, an open detention bridging visa and a community release bridging visa.

With an open detention bridging visa:

- accommodation and daily requirements are provided by the Department;
- the visa holder can leave the centre between the hours (for example) 7.00 am and 7.00 pm;
- the visa holder must sign out and in to the hostel when departing and returning;
- eligibility for permission to work is available on the terms contained in the current Bridging Visa E;
- a visa holder who obtains employment must pay a fee for accommodation and board; and
- a visa holder is eligible for Asylum Seekers' Assistance on the terms currently available to other asylum seekers and, if granted, a fee for accommodation is deducted prior to payment to the visa holder.

With a community release bridging visa:

- the visa holder resides at an approved designated address;
- the visa holder must notify the Department of any change of address within 48 hours;
- the visa holder must report to the Department at regular intervals specified by the case officer;
- the visa holder or the nominated close family may be required to pay a bond to the Department or sign a recognisance with the Department;
- if called upon to do so, the visa holder shall present to the case officer within 24 hours;

- the visa holder is required to sign an undertaking in writing that he or she shall comply with the conditions of the visa and, in the event that a condition of the visa is breached, may be returned to detention;
- eligibility for permission to work is available on the terms contained in the current Bridging Visa E; and
- eligibility for Asylum Seekers' Assistance is on the terms currently available to other asylum seekers.

The Australian criminal justice system already provides a range of release options with varying degrees of supervision for those on bail or parol or probation. The options include reporting to police or other officials, living and remaining in a specified place or district, home detention and electronic monitoring. These same, well tried options could be made available for asylum seekers released from detention. The conditions on the visas proposed by the Human Rights and Equal Opportunity Commission seem unnecessarily restrictive, making the options attached to the visas very narrow. A better approach involves complete flexibility in determining the appropriate conditions to be attached to a visa. No person should be subjected to more restriction of freedom than is necessary (Refugee Convention article 31, 1951). Each person should be individually assessed and, where some restriction is considered necessary, for example, for one of the reasons relevant to a decision to continue detention, then it should be the least appropriate restriction necessary for the individual asylum seeker.

Fourth, any asylum seeker who breaches the conditions set for his or her release without good reason may be returned to detention and should not be eligible to reapply for release for a period of 30 days from the time of return to detention. Further if circumstances change so that an asylum seeker who was released comes within one of the five categories of person who may be detained, the person may be returned to detention. Where an asylum seeker is returned to detention, his or her detention must be reviewed before the completion of a 30 day period. In considering release the departmental officer may consider each of the criteria applicable in relation to an initial decision to detain.

Finally, any asylum seeker detained beyond the initial period of 30 days may seek review of the decision to continue detention. A departmental officer may review at any time and must do so at least every 30 days. An asylum seeker may also seek independent external review of the necessity of continued detention beyond the 30 day initial period and of the necessity and appropriateness of any restrictions imposed as conditions for release. Where the review is undertaken by a tribunal, the Federal Court should be able to review the decision of the tribunal on a point of law.

This basic model is a workable alternative to the present system that meets all the principles I have enunciated. It respects the human rights of asylum seekers. It offers appropriate protection to the Australian community. It is also, coincidentally, far less expensive than the present system, a far lesser drain on taxpayers' resources. There is no agreed method for calculating cost but on any basis the cost is great and growing. The Human Rights and Equal Opportunity Commission reported various estimates of the costs of the detention system during the 1990s:

- in 1994, according to a parliamentary committee report, $55.64 per person per day at Port Hedland, $58.49 at Villawood and about $200 at other centres
- in September 1997, according to a ministerial statement to Parliament, $161.77 per person per day at Port Hedland and $111.11 at other centres
- in 1998, according to the Australian National Audit Office, $69 per person per day in 1994 95, increasing by more than 50 per cent in the following year to $105 per person per day (HREOC, 1998:237).

The Conference of Leaders of Religious Institutes, NSW (2001, 3.8.1) provided a telling comparison of the costs per person per day of detention and of supervised release in the community, as calculated by a NSW parliamentary committee in June 2000:

- Prison maximum security $177.43
- medium security $161.35
- minimum security $121.09
- Community release parole $5.39
- probation $3.94
- home detention $58.83
- hostel $5.89.

No immigration detention centre is comparable to a minimum security prison. The cost per person per day would be similar to that in a medium or maximum security prison. The cost of an alternative release option would be more than the costs shown here for the criminal justice system because most convicted persons released under this scheme have their own homes to return to. Asylum seekers would not and so housing costs would be in addition to those shown. Nonetheless, there remains a very significant difference. Community options are far less expensive.

These estimates were calculated before the socalled Pacific Solution was devised and implemented. The cost of this approach is unknown but it has been estimated at $500 million this year, far more than the disclosed cost of the onshore system. The alternative model offers real savings to taxpayers as a bonus on top of the more ethical, more humane dimensions.

The alternative approach I have described here is similar to the approaches taken successfully in most other western countries (Nicholas, 2001). In Sweden, for example, where this kind of approach has been taken for many years, the average stay in a detention centre is a mere 47 days (Mitchell, 2001). One argument against a release scheme is that it will not deter other asylum seekers. But detention solely as a means to deter others is unacceptable and a violation of the Refugee Convention and of human rights law. And in any event there is no evidence that the various deterrent steps taken by Australian governments over the last decade have worked. Another argument is that released asylum seekers will abscond. Careful assessment before release and appropriate reporting requirements after release will minimise the risk of absconding. Experience in the United States, where release of asylum seekers is routine pending determination of status, is that few abscond. Indeed in one pilot monitoring scheme 95 per cent met every reporting requirement (Nicholas, 2001:4).

Conclusion

The present situation cannot continue. It is unsustainable on practical grounds. It simply is not working. It is expensive. It is destroying Australia's good name. It is distorting Australian aid priorities and warping development patterns in small poor Pacific Island states. But far graver than any of these facts, present policy is violating human rights.

Contrary to what is said by many of our national political leaders and many media commentators change towards fairness and decency in refugee policy is possible. It is necessary if we are to restore our integrity in our own eyes and in the eyes of the world. All it will take is political will and a little bit of decency.

REFERENCES

Conference of Leaders of Religious Institutes (NSW) (2001) Policy proposal for adjustments to Australia's asylum seeking process, 13 June 2001, http://www.refugeecouncil.org.au/html/current_issues/ alternativesreligious.html.

Human Rights and Equal Opportunity Commission (1998), Those who've come across the seas: detention of unauthorised arrivals. Commonwealth of Australia: Sydney.

Mackay, H. (2002), 'Shame on us all', *Sydney Morning Herald*, 30 Mar 2002, p. 28.

Mitchell, G. (2001), Asylum seekers in Sweden, unpublished August.

Nicholas, A. W. (2001), Protecting refugees: alternatives to a policy of mandatory detention, unpublished.

Oxfam Community Aid Abroad (2002), Adrift in the Pacific: The implications of Australia's Pacific refugee solution, February, http://www.oxfam.org.au/campaigns/refugees/pacificsol ution/

United Nations High Commission for Refugees (2001), Article 31 of the 1951 Convention relating to the Status of Refugees, Geneva Expert Roundtable, 89 Nov 2001, http://www.unhcr.bg/global_consult/article_31_1951cr sr_en.pdf

United Nations High Commissioner for Refugees (1986), Executive Committee Conclusion on Detention of Refugees and Asylum Seekers, No. 44.

ENDNOTE

1. The Charter was endorsed by the Australian Council of Churches, Australian Council of Social Service, Australian Red Cross, Federation of Ethnic Communities Councils of Australia, Human Rights and Equal Opportunity Commission, Immigration Advice and Rights Centre (NSW & Victoria), International Commission of Jurists, International Social Service, Legal Aid Commission of NSW, Migration Institute of Australia, National Legal Aid, Refugee Advice and Casework Service (NSW & Victoria), Refugee Council of Australia, Service for the Treatment and Rehabilitation of Torture and Trauma Survivors (NSW), South Brisbane Immigration and Community Legal Service, St Vincent de Paul Society and Uniya.

CHAPTER SIX

BORDER PROTECTION AND DETENTION

JACQUELINE EVERETT

Introduction

Australia has a history of search and rescue. Remember Stuart Diver the young man buried after the Thredbo landslide? The whole country sat glued to television sets and rejoiced when he was found alive. Australians have been searching and rescuing since whites first came here. That is why the *Tampa* story is such a blot on our history and so out of keeping with our national ethos. We have always pulled out all stops to save people lost or in peril.

The *Tampa* incident changed that.

'I will decide who comes to Australia,' announced Prime Minister Howard. Australia cheered and backed Mr Howard. Compassion for those on board — the children, the traumatised people fleeing persecution — was lost. The majority of Australians were regarded as supporting the Government stance.

Captain Rinnan, master of the *Tampa,* a Norwegian merchant ship responded to the Australian Government's request to rescue the asylum seekers off a disabled Indonesian vessel. He conveyed them to Australian waters and was refused permission to dock at Christmas Island. The result was a standoff that lasted for six days.

The asylum seekers were taken to Nauru, a small bankrupt island in the Pacific. The unaccompanied children and the families were then taken to New Zealand where their claims were processed and all were found to be refugees. The remaining asylum seekers were assessed and all but one were found to be refugees. The then Minister for Immigration, Philip Ruddock, scoured the world to find other countries to take them.

The *Tampa* incident is now part of history.

Afterwards, a raft of laws were rushed through Federal Parliament by the Government with barely a dissenting voice heard from the Labor opposition. We neatly excised from our migration zone Christmas Island, the Ashmore and Cartier Reefs and the Keeling (Cocos) Islands. But equally importantly, we made it an offence for any ship to rescue endangered people at sea in Australian waters without first notifying our navy. What happened to the International Law of the Sea?

Now let's flash back to October 8 2001. SIEV 4 (Suspected Illegal Entry Vessel) overladen with SUNCs (Suspected Unlawful NonCitizens — for us, they are not even people, just acronyms) makes a perilous journey towards Christmas Island and the Australian navy orders it to turn back to Indonesia.

The boat continues ahead and to force it to stop, not one, but four canon blasts and 23 rounds of medium (50mm) shells are fired across its bows by H M A S Adelaide. It takes a full 45 minutes to fire off all that ammunition. It is not difficult to imagine the fear of these already traumatised people on board. They hold their children aloft to indicate they have precious cargo. The rest of that story is also history — lies and vilification of those asylum seekers by Australian politicians.

There was no statement of concern for the fear these people had experienced 'under fire', no mention of the danger the children were in, none of the normal responses to a perilous neardisaster such as this.

Instead they were denigrated, defamed and debased. They were forcibly transported to Manus Island, Papua New Guinea, where the media, lawyers and anyone else who could check the accuracy of the accusations made by the politicians were totally barred from speaking with them.

Hiding asylum seekers on Manus Island and Nauru is one step further than locking them in desert camps in Australia. Ordinary Australians are denied the chance even to see asylum seekers. Why? Because if we do not see them, we cannot empathise with them. We cannot let our natural instincts of compassion and humanity take over. If we do not see them we do not know they are just like us. If we do not see them, we will not know that Muslims are very little different from Christians, Jews, Buddhists, atheists or anyone else we care to label.

Australia has a long-standing policy of mandatory detention for people who arrive whether by plane or boat, without the required documents, including visas. We are the only western country to do this. In 1998 the Human Rights and Equal Opportunity Commission found

Australia's openended mandatory detention policy in violation of international law. As at January 2004 we have six centres in Australia where every man, woman and child who arrives onshore in Australia without the correct documents is placed in mandatory detention.

Australians have a history of decency, a history of standing up for values. Are we meanspirited, do we disregard human rights? Not when judged by our historical record of taking refugees — 650,000 since World War II — but we do have a real problem with our current leaders on both sides of the political fence.

The Government has been covering up the true facts and running a misinformation programme based on innuendos, halftruths and absolute lies, using inflammatory words ('illegal immigrants', 'queue jumpers', 'economic migrants' and 'selfselectors') until the very word 'refugee' has now taken on a pejorative meaning. The cycle continues and the Government reacts to negative public opinion by maintaining or even strengthening its 'tough on refugees' stance.

Australia has a humanitarian programme through which we receive an average of 12,000 people per year and 4,000 of these places are for refugees arriving onshore. Onshore asylum seekers are those who arrive without appropriate visa requirements and these are the only refugees that Australia is legally obliged to protect under international law. We do not always fill this quota.

As a signatory to the 1951 Convention on the Status of Refugees, Australia assesses whether or not those claiming refugee status fit the convention definition. They must have fled their own country because of persecution 'for reasons of race, religion, nationality, membership of a particular social group or political opinion'. They must have a genuine fear of returning because of one or more of those reasons.

Mandatory Detention Policies in Context

It was Gerry Hand, Labor Minister for Immigration, who was determined to put a stop to the second wave — or ripple — of boat people who began arriving from China, Vietnam and Cambodia in 1989. Up until that time we had welcomed refugees homeless after World War II; we had received 52 boats after the fall of Saigon in 1975 (the first ripple) and some 20,000 Chinese students after the Tiananmen Square confrontation.

Labor's Nick Bolkus followed Gerry Hand and then Philip Ruddock, all three equally zealous in their support of mandatory detention and great detractors of the courts whom they regard as soft on asylum seekers. With bipartisan approval successive Australian governments have been outspoken in their belief that locking up asylum seekers sends out what they consider a strong message aimed at deterring others from setting out for Australia.

There is no consideration of our international responsibilities as a treaty member, no consideration for the human rights of those we lock up arbitrarily. In the third ripple of boat arrivals, between the beginning of January and the end of August 2001, 3685 asylum seekers arrived; 2946 in 2000 and 3726 in 1999 (DIMIA, 2004). Hardly a deluge considering that Australia actively solicits and receives between 75,000 and 80,000 migrants every year, mostly under family reunion or special skills categories. This year, and for the next three years, Australia is aiming to attract 105,000 immigrants.

A brief period of initial mandatory detention is generally considered acceptable worldwide. International law and practice recognises this is permissible for reasons of identification, public health, safety and security. What is not acceptable on a human rights basis is extending mandatory detention indefinitely. Nor is it acceptable under the rule of law to deny individual assessment of the very need to detain and the complete denial of judicial review of detention which extends beyond that initial period. In Australia, some asylum seekers — including those born here — have been kept for as many as five years before being released into the community. Others have been deported after four years.

The UK receives 84,000 applications for asylum each year. There are estimated to be three million people inside the European Union without permission and around 5 million in the United States. Australia averages about 13,000. Consider those 4000 arriving by boat. The Manly ferry carries 1,200 people. So we are talking about less than four Manly ferry loads. Yet in Australia there is governmental and public hysteria about border protection. In fact, research in 1999 showed that the Australian people believed there were 70 times more asylum seekers arriving uninvited than the actual figure.

Consider that it is estimated that there were some 53,000 overstayers within our community in June 1999. These are people who arrived on valid visas and have simply stayed once their visas expired. If you want to point a finger at illegal immigrants, these might be a more legitimate target — though that is not what I am advocating. These 53,000 made a conscious decision to stay, knowing their presence was against the law.

Asylum seekers are not illegal immigrants until they have exhausted every legal avenue — they came under an international treaty which Australia signed willingly and which grants them the right to make a refugee claim.

Until the Pacific Solution was devised, an onshore arriver without the correct documents was assessed through a three tiered system. Those who are currently in detention in Australia fall under this regime. I will deal with Nauru and Manus Island later.

First of all, only 10 percent of those arriving onshore and seeking asylum are accepted at the first stage, a round of interviews by DIMIA staff (Department of Immigration, Multicultural and Indigenous Affairs). A further 16 percent (it used to be 17 percent, then dropped to 10 percent) of those who failed at this round of interviews are accepted after a merits review by the RRT (Refugee Review Tribunal). This figure is higher than previously because of the increased number of Iraqis and Afghans.

There will be one person on this 'tribunal'. This one person will not be a judge, trained to analyse evidence, but a lay person. The tribunal member may have legal training, may even be well-versed in the politics, geography and culture of the region the asylum seeker came from — but that is not strictly necessary. His or her placement might have been for political reasons.

I have heard of a tribunal member who asked why there were so many barbers in Algeria — he had never heard of Berbers, the indigenous people. I have heard worse anecdotes of tribunal member ignorance, but that is not the point. I spoke on a panel with an RRT member recently and he told the audience some of the methods an RRT member uses to catch asylum seekers out in lies. He did not mention any ways an RRT member employs to flesh out the truth nor help the asylum seeker to make his case.

It takes very careful work to draw out the stories of these traumatised people, and tribunal members appear to be encouraged to see their role as adversarial. Many asylum seekers have experienced interrogations by military or religious police in the countries from which they have fled and often find tribunal member questioning such an uncomfortable experience they are unable to answer questions accurately.

So now we have 26 percent of asylum seekers accepted through the two tiers of assessment. Canada, which has a similar two tier process, accepts 60 percent at this stage. More than twice as many as Australia through two almost identical processes.

Could it really be that twice as many genuine refugees find their way to Canada as arrive in Australia? I doubt it; I suspect it is the attitude of the Canadian government itself filtering down to those who make the hands on decision that causes these different percentage results. Canada is a country that takes its human rights obligations seriously.

Failure at this stage leaves only the court system. Australia has trimmed and doctored our original Migration Act until, with its new privative clause of 2001 to constrain review, it is extremely difficult for an asylum seeker to succeed in this third stage in our refugee assessment system. Class and representative proceedings have been banned in migration cases and there have even been attempts to place time limits on application to the High Court.

But it is very difficult to explain to an asylum seeker that he is not a refugee. His brother might have been executed by the soldiers of Saddam Hussein, his two young nephews fresh from national might have been tortured. He may have been the one who had to identify the bodies.

The family may have press cuttings to prove these tragedies. They may have fled without even gathering their belongings on a tip-off from a government employee and, with their new baby and their five older children, managed to get to the Jordanian border.

Are they refugees? Have they suffered enough at the hands of Saddam Hussein's repressive regime?

This family spent four years in Jordan and Syria on expired visas. They had no legal right to stay and moved on to Malaysia, Indonesia and then to Australia. Australia has rejected their claim, not on the basis of their refugee claim but because they spent time in a 'safe' country before they came to Australia.

Since we cannot send Iraqis back because Australia has no diplomatic relations with Iraq, they must remain in detention. They have been locked up for two and a half years — in Curtin, Port Hedland and Villawood. Their teenage sons have made serious suicide attempts and the 16 year old has been in psychiatric hospitals three times.

Until May 2002, the situation was the same for Afghans as for Iraqis, they could not be sent back, however, the Australian Government has determined that the situation is now clear in Afghanistan, we have established diplomatic relations and the first planeload returned under the auspices of the International Organisation for Migration (IOM) in May (Williams, 2002).

For the third largest group of asylum seekers in Australia, Iranians, there are options. The Iranian Government does not accept failed asylum seekers unless they sign documents to say they are returning voluntarily. This poses problems for the Government. The fact that Australia rejects their claims does not convince the Iranian asylum seekers themselves that they are not refugees.

If they are too afraid to go back, they must remain prisoners in a detention camp in Australia.

Impact of Long-term Detention

Families such as the above must watch as their teenage sons becoming more and more angry and closer and closer to the edge of suicide; as their teenage daughters who have been through the trauma of riots and paralysing fear, become humiliated by incontinence day and night; as their younger children withdraw from social contact, have night terrors after all they have witnessed in detention, wet their beds, are offered minimal schooling and sleep away the days or sit mindlessly in front of a television set. All these are documented symptoms of child asylum seekers.

All the long-term detainee children I have met are suffering as the children above. I have no qualifications to assess them, but my colleagues and I have collected affidavits and there is a pattern common to children in all the detention centres. Woomera, Curtain, Port Hedland and Villawood. It is all the same.

Australia is also a signatory to the Convention against Torture and Other Cruel, Inhuman or Degrading Treatment or Punishment (1984) (Torture Convention). This not only prevents Australia from returning people who suffered torture, but also obliges us to treat those on our shores in a way that does not constitute torture.

Common forms of torture include sleep deprivation, use of psychotropic drugs, psychological abuse, isolation and solitary detention, beatings, exposure to heat and cold and being forced to watch the brutalisation of family and friends. All these have occurred in our detention centres.

The Minister for Immigration, Ruddock, publicly blamed asylum seekers for the psychological problems their children experienced and declared that it is irresponsible of them to have brought their children all the way across the world just to make an asylum claim in Australia. He seemed to have forgotten that the countries they travel through are not signatories to the Convention, and therefore are under no international law obligation to offer protection.

Further, Ruddock said long-term detainees remain in detention by their own choice because they insist on continuing through the court system. They simply refuse to take the decision of the umpire. But it is very difficult for many of these people to accept they are not refugees simply because an RRT member tells them they are not. The people I know in detention have an absolutely morbid fear of being returned. They find it impossible to consider going back and beg to be sent anywhere but where they came from.

Quarantining

Screening out is a sinister practice considered a form of quarantine in the medical sense, where those who are untainted by knowledge are kept apart from those who know what legal rights are available. The idea is that those who do not know should be kept ignorant until they can be returned to the country from which they fled.

To avoid being screened out, an asylum seeker has to say the magic words. Something like: 'I was subjected to conventionbased persecution in my own country, I have a great fear of returning, I am seeking the protection of Australia and I want a lawyer.'

It is especially difficult for a child under 18 who arrives without his or her normal caregiver — UAM in DIMIA acronym parlance — to know what to say, because children do not network and take part in information exchanges on the trip to Australia in the same way that adults do. Often, even wives of previous arrivals who arrive here onshore with their children will be screened out as they are culturally more withdrawn than the men and do not mix with others so they do not learn the magic words of asylum. Yet, if a woman's husband has been accepted as a refugee, the wife and children will be given refugee status too. Why are they screened out then if their husbands are in the community on visas?

The worst stories belong to the unaccompanied children and their sadness, confusion and feelings of powerlessness shames us more than any other aspect of Australia's detention policy. These children cry alone at night, uncomforted. There numbers have been as high as 300, although now they are down to single digits.

I met a number of young boys and one girl in Woomera at the end of 2001. She is 15. She has a sweet face and wears a hand-embroidered headscarf and traditional Afghani clothes. She and her 11 year old brother are orphans. Their mother died some time ago and their father was taken by the Taliban. They believe he is dead. They had been living with their grandparents who feared for the children's lives and their futures and decided to get the children to safety. They gave them to the people smugglers — seen by asylum seekers as saviours. The children had no idea where they were going.

When they arrived in Australia they had one interview with DIMIA. After this, each morning this girl would dress carefully, take her chair outside the donga (aluminium containers used as accommodation) and wait to be called for another interview like all the other people. But she and her brother were never called. They had been screened out. They had not said the magic words of asylum.

These two children waited every day for almost six months, then, miraculously, they were back in the system. When I asked her how she was managing, she began to cry. She told how she had no-one to talk to, but she was desperately worried. Her grandparents' last words as she and her brother left were: 'We will try to raise the money and follow you, so we can take care of you.'

She had heard that a boat had sunk and she was certain her grandparents had drowned. She had no way of finding out if they were still in Afghanistan as there is no way of communicating with Afghanistan at all. She sobbed and I put my arms around her — I have a daughter of the same age.

She told me that she cried often in her bed at night, and this was the first time anyone was with her who could put their arms around her and comfort her. She said I was the first person who had touched her since she had been in Australia. She did not know she could have access to a doctor, a nurse or a counsellor. No one had told her.

These children are out of detention now, in care in Adelaide, I believe. They were amongst the first five children to be released during the period of hunger strikes and lip sewing. They were locked away in the desert of Woomera for about eight months yet there is a mechanism within the Migration Act for an unaccompanied child to be got out of detention on a bridging visa. If this is possible, why are they locked up in the first place? Surely health checks can be done in a few days.

Children could not seriously be considered a security threat, could they? These children have been neither charged nor convicted of any crime. They have merely been sent to safety by family who could only afford one fare. They are alone and of all asylum seekers are the ones who are in the most desperate need of humanitarian assistance.

In Port Hedland I know an 18 year old Afghan boy. The Taliban took his father and the family has not heard from him since, then his brother was taken. The Taliban do this, they come into a village and kill or kidnap. His mother and extended family sent him to Australia alone. He was 16 then and has now spent more than two years locked up. He was in Villawood but took part in a hunger strike and was sent to Port Hedland at 4 am in the morning on a chartered plane. On arrival he was locked in a solitary confinement cell with the air conditioning turned down and no blanket. He felt very cold. He told me he could only roll up tightly to try to keep warm.

He cries now and he stutters. He is desolate and has no way of contacting any of his family. He fears that he will be returned and is terrified of the consequences. He is scathing of the Australian Government's offer of money to return. He has tried to trace his mother through the Red Cross, but there is no trace to follow.

He is Hazarah, an ethnic minority descended from Genghis Khan's army and persecuted for centuries. He is huge and when he cried I put my arms around him. He cried with his head resting on my head, his body racked with sobs. He told me he still cries every night. This boy has been rejected as a refugee. I believe he will be sent back to Afghanistan now and I doubt whether he will ever recover from his years in Australia.

What Options?

Since September 11 2001, the world's fear of terrorists has ensured that it is impossible for the Government to find a third country for failed asylum seekers. Iraqis and Palestinians cannot be returned so we have a situation that means they must be detained indefinitely. This surely means that for them, at least, the then Minister's, Ruddock, claim that 'nobody is forced to remain in detention' is not correct (Ruddock, 2001).

Under s417 of the Migration Act, 1957 (Cth) the Minister may substitute the Refugee Review Tribunal (RRT) decision with a decision more favourable to the applicants by granting a protection visa or some other class of visa when there are humanitarian reasons for protection even though the applicant has not been found to be a refugee. The Minister has used this discretion in hundreds of cases. Most of the detainees I see in Villawood are now at this stage of writing to the Minister or beyond it.

The result often takes many months to come.

A further option is reopening an asylum seekers case in the light of changed circumstances. This is done under s48 of the Migration Act and requires the Minister's permission. Such an application amounts to a virtual reassessment of the asylum seeker's claims under the current country conditions of their homeland.

The lawfulness of mandatory detention is a contentious issue. Human rights lawyers argue that it is not lawful. The High Court considered this issue in Chu Kheng Lim and Others v The Minister For Immigration (1992) and found that while the Constitution grants exclusive judicial power to the designated courts, limited authority to detain an alien in custody can be conferred on the executive. However if this detention is punitive, it contravenes Chapter III of the Constitution which states that the judicial power of the Commonwealth rests exclusively in the courts which the Constitution itself designates.

Ruddock (2002) stated in the Medical Journal of Australia, in response to a previously published research paper by Dr Aamer Sultan, an Iraqi detained in Villawood Immigration Detention Centre (IDC), and Kevin Sullivan, a psychologist formerly employed at Villawood IDC, that 'Detention is not arbitrary. It is humane and is not designed to be punitive' (p. 85).

Yet clearly it is arbitrary when there is no reasonable way an Iraqi or Palestinian can return home.

Detention as Deterrent

Ruddock frequently stated that Australia must send a strong message to potential asylum seekers that we are tough on uninvited arrivals. He saw mandatory detention as being part of this deterrent message. In Hansard, February 19, 2002, his intentions are clearly noted. He says that by passing laws to 'strengthen our territorial integrity' Australia 'has been successful in deterring potential illegal immigrants from making their way to Australia' (p. 420).

These statements illustrate the doubtfulness about the constitutional validity of legislation authorising administrative detention without allowing access to the courts (as is now the situation since the inclusion of the privative clause) because they indicate that detention may be neither relevant nor incidental to the processing of an asylum seeker's claims but is a deterrent.

The post-*Tampa* Pacific Solution means that asylum seekers no longer arrive on Australian soil. It amounts to the forcible transfer of people across national boundaries to be dumped in poor island states paid to accept people Australia chooses not to take. Nauru is not even a party to the Refugee Convention and therefore is under no obligation not to return them to their country of persecution. There are currently constitutional challenges in train in both Papua New Guinea and Nauru to determine whether those two countries may legally accept asylum seekers under these terms.

A new detention facility has been built on Christmas Island — no longer part of Australia for immigration purposes and therefore not subject to Australia's obligations under the Convention. Does this mean that technically those who arrive there have no access to Australian courts and will simply be able to be turned straight around and returned to their country of persecution in the light of the excision of Christmas Island from Australian territory for immigration purposes? But perhaps there will be a legal challenge to this playing with the boundaries.

Children in Detention

The issue of children in detention is the most emotionally charged of all.

It is an odd irony that in Australia our state laws provide for mandatory reporting of suspected child abuse by professionals, and at the other end of the perspective, the mandatory locking up of child asylum seekers. We call both these government policy — one protects and one destroys.

We recognise the vulnerability of our own children but if these children are not our own we are prepared to put them in circumstances which can leave them damaged for life. Can we afford to do this? In dollar terms this is an expensive exercise — some $115 per day per person — but in terms of humanity, the cost is incalculable.

I believe that in mid 2002, there were only 153 children in detention in Australia, down from some 582 at the end of November 2001. The Pacific Solution has certainly taken these children away from our gaze and minimised the numbers in Australia. At that time on Nauru there were 243 children, on Manus Island, 125. It is impossible to gain access to those places, so we have no idea how children there are faring.

On the one hand we are told that the Government's tough stance has been successful, yet more detention centres have been built — on Christmas Island, at Port Augusta in South Australia, in Darwin and in Singleton, NSW.

Currently, children in Australia are mostly in desert camps — detainees with children are rarely transferred to Villawood now — it is too easy for ordinary people to get in and see what is happening to them and to hear their stories. I think I am correct in saying that since the publicity caused by Shayan Badraie's case in August 2001, the only families with children sent to Villawood have been short-term stayers about to be deported.

Shayan was the six year old boy whose story was told on the ABC's Four Corners programme in August 2001. A hidden camera showed Shayan with his parents and sister (born in Woomera) and told of his diagnosis of acute post traumatic stress syndrome. The little boy had experienced riots, water canon, tear gas and witnessed self mutilation and suicide attempts in Woomera, but it was the sight of a man slitting his wrist, with the blood spurting and collapsing apparently dead, that finally caused Shayan to give up eating, drinking and talking altogether.

This little boy is now out in the community with his mother and sister. His family's case, rejected at the RRT and before a single judge in the Federal Court, has now been heard on appeal at the Full Federal Court where the appeal was unanimously upheld by the three judges of the full bench.

Further, the family made a complaint to the Human Rights and Equal Opportunity Commission in August 2002 and the preliminary findings by Professor Alice Tay, president of the Commission, state that the Department of Immigration has committed breaches of human rights in Shayan's case.

Is this an issue of child abuse? Using NSW law as an example, The Children and Young Person's Care and Protection Act, 1998 (NSW) states that everyone has a role to play in ensuring the safety, welfare and wellbeing of children and young people in NSW and that when any professional sees a child at risk of harm, she or he is legally required to report such concerns to the Department of Community Service (DoCS). Yet every child in detention in Australia must surely be at risk. Quite simply Australia's detention system ill treats children — detainee children are being institutionally abused by a statute.

Under our mandatory detention system there is no regard for the right of children to grow, learn and develop in a supporting environment. Surely it is up to every one of us to take all possible steps to make sure that this systematic child abuse arising from current Government policy is stopped immediately.

Under the Refugee Guardianship Act, the Minister for Immigration is the legal guardian of the unaccompanied children in detention. This means that Minister Ruddock was a perpetrator of the abuse of children by the very fact that his department, which administers Federal legislation and locks these children up, is also their guardian.

How can this be?

He may not be personally terrifying them in the night in the persona of a guards conducting a raid nor personally subjecting them to the horrific sights that confront them almost daily, but it is his responsibility to keep them safe and surely wilful blindness is no defence. Every day, it appears, he breaches his duty of care as their guardian.

It is not necessary to be a psychologist to see that detention is an evil for all the children incarcerated. The body of evidence must surely be indisputable.

I have just read the diary of a teenage girl who arrived in Australia at the age of 13 with hopes of being a doctor. The diary was as we would expect — a tragic litany of crushed hopes, confusion and pleas to God to save all the detainees. She could not understand why she and her family were locked up, why Australia did not believe her family's claims, why everyday people were released, but never her family, when their history of persecution was as strong.

She was deported last week. She is now 16 and has been through riots in Woomera and Port Hedland. She has had no schooling worthy of the definition of education since she arrived in Australia and is shattered and bitter that on her return she will be so far behind her peers that she has no chance of catching up. She may not even be allowed to return to school as it is not yet clear in what way her family will be penalised for seeking asylum in Australia. Her mother, the family member with the refugee claim, was detained for four hours by police at the airport when the family returned and has now been ordered to appear before court — we do not know whether it was the punitive Revolutionary Court.

This young girl believed she lost her chance at life through her lack of education. She thought she would be able to do some sewing to earn money. Do Australians regard this as a fair go? Iran is a country in deep financial distress, seeking aid money from the global community. Australia is a western country, which can afford to be generous to children such as her. The very least we could have done was provide her with adequate education before we shipped her back.

I made a notification to DOCS about the mental state of the three children in this family. An immediate assessment was made and the recommendation was that this young girl was on the edge of psychosis. The recommendation was that the mother and children should be released immediately into the community.

The department refused to do so.

The family made the only decision possible: to take their damaged children and return to the country of their persecution. The mother was fearful of return, but she could no longer watch the disintegration of her children.

Conclusion

Is Australia really a mean-spirited nation, lacking compassion? Is the perception of enhanced sovereignty and border protection really worth sacrificing the human rights of all detainees? Will our detention policy be seen by future generations as shaming, an abandonment of the rule of law and something for which a future Prime Minister will be moved to say sorry?

This current pitiless policy diminishes us all.

REFERENCES

ABC (2001), 'The Inside Story' Reported by Debbie Whitmont, Four Corners, 13 Aug 2001. Chu Kheng Lim & Ors v Minister for Immigration, Local Government & Ethnic Affairs (1992) 110 ALR 97.

DIMIA (Department of Immigration, Multicultural and Indigenous Affairs), (2004), Fact Sheet 74a. Boat Arrival Details, http://www.immi.gov.au/facts/74a_boatarrivals.htm

HREOC (Human Rights and Equal Opportunity Commisssion), (1998), Those who've come across the seas: detention of unauthorised arrivals. Commonwealth of Australia: Sydney.

HREOC (2002), Report of an inquiry into a complaint by Mr Mohammed Badraie on behalf of his son Shayan regarding acts or practices of the Commonwealth of Australia (the Department of Immigration, Multicultural and Indigenous Affairs) HREOC Report No. 25,
http://www.hreoc.gov.au/human_rights/human_rights_reports/hrc_25.html

Ruddock, P. (2001), General Synod of the Anglican Church of Australian, 27 July 2001, Brisbane.
Ruddock, P. (2002), 'Letter to the Editor', Medical Journal of Australia, 176 (2), 85.
Ruddock, P. (2002), House of Representatives, Official Hansard, No. 2, 2002, Tuesday 19 Feb 2002, http://www.aph.gov.au/hansard/reps/dailys/dr190202.pdf
Williams, B. (2002), 'Afghans return home nursing hatred for Australia', Sydney Morning Herald, 13 May 2002, p. 4.

CHAPTER SEVEN

REFUGEE RIGHTS OVERBOARD

THE *TAMPA* CASE AND THE NEED FOR A NEW GLOBAL PERSPECTIVE

MICHAEL HEAD

At the height of the *Tampa* affair, Prime Minister John Howard made it clear that for his government the central issue was the defence of the national state. 'We cannot surrender our right as a sovereign country to control our borders,' he said, 'and we cannot have a situation where people can come to this country when they choose' (A Current Affair, 28/08/01).

During the November 2001 election campaign, he reiterated this theme: 'We decide who comes to this country and the circumstances in which they come'. His statement became the Liberal Party's central election slogan.

This poses an issue of principle point-blank: the defence of national sovereignty necessarily conflicts with the rights of refugees fleeing oppression. Critics of the Government's response may argue for a more humane refugee policy, yet accept one overriding principle, that at some point the state must set limits to the inflow of people. It follows from this proposition, however, that if those limits are threatened physically, the armed forces must be called in to enforce them. Moreover, if need be, in order to protect the government and the military from legal challenge, longheld legal rights and civil liberties must be sacrificed.

That is exactly what happened in the *Tampa* case. This raises, I suggest, the necessity for a completely opposed principle: recognition of the fundamental democratic right of people to freedom of movement and residence on a global scale. This view rejects the present official artificial distinction between refugees and socalled economic immigrants — those who simply seek a better life for themselves and their children, usually in order to escape poverty, exploitation, discrimination and armed conflict. This distinction, I argue, is not only inhumane, but ultimately untenable in an increasingly globalised, economically unequal, socially-polarised and war torn world.

By deploying naval warships to confront and turn back leaking refugee boats, and remove asylum seekers to remote Pacific islands, the Australian Government has set a number of dangerous and far-reaching legal and political precedents. But the implications of the *Tampa* affair go further. While the mobilisation of the armed forces to physically prevent refugees from exercising their rights, under international and domestic law, to apply for asylum makes a mockery of the Government's claim to abide by the 1951 Convention Relating to the Status of Refugees, the military operation also highlights the inherent flaws in the Convention itself. Rather than enshrining a right to asylum, the Convention upholds national sovereignty, effectively permitting governments to turn away refugees.

This chapter will argue that the *Tampa* affair demonstrates the need for a radically different perspective, one based on global citizenship. The first section examines the legality and political context of the Government's actions in the *Tampa* case. The second points to the underlying causes of the *Tampa* crisis in the global plight of refugees and the defects of the current international framework. The third and final part poses the need for root and branch change.

Tampa, Legal Rights and the Courts

It appears that Captain Arne Rinnan, the master of the Norwegian freighter M V *Tampa,* displayed more concern for the survival, welfare and basic rights of the 433 Afghan refugees rescued by the *Tampa* on 26 August 2001 than the Australian government. In accordance with the norms of international humanitarian assistance, Rinnan responded to the refugees' distress calls and sought to ferry them to the nearest safe port.' By contrast, the Howard Government seized upon the plight of the *Tampa* refugees to demonise asylum seekers, whip up xenophobia and assert a dramatically expanded version of executive power, above and beyond the laws passed by parliament.

Led by Prime Minister Howard and Immigration Minister Philip Ruddock, the Government deployed Special Air Services (SAS) troops to prevent the asylum seekers landing in a safe harbour (at Christmas Island), detain them on the deck of the container ship and ultimately transfer them to the HMAS *Manoora*, a naval troop carrier, for transportation to far-distant Nauru.

The ministers were aware that they probably lacked any legislative power to do so. They attempted to rush retrospective legislation, the Border Protection Bill, 2001, through parliament to authorise their actions, but it was initially defeated in the Senate. The clear purpose of the SAS operation was to evade the Migration Act, which requires government officers to detain all 'unlawful' arrivals. Under the 1999 'border protection' amendments to the Act, officials who board refugee vessels, even on the high seas, are obliged to bring the people on board ashore, to be placed in detention (Migration Act, 1957 ss. 189, 245).

On the federal cabinet's instructions, various steps were taken to ensure that the *Tampa* rescuees could not contact lawyers to challenge the legality of the Government's conduct or seek their release from the ship. Government leaders were determined to prevent them from applying for refugee status and protection visas. In fact, when their actions were challenged in the Federal Court by the Victorian Council of Civil Liberties and Melbourne solicitor Eric Vadarlis (2001), the Government's representatives admitted as much.

According to the agreed facts in the case:

> The ship has been forbidden by Australian authorities from proceeding any closer to Christmas Island and from entering the port ... The effect of the continuing presence of the SAS officers is that the captain and crew are unlikely to attempt to move the ship into the port. This is a consequence desired by the Australian government ...

The evidence justifies an inference that many of the rescuees would, if entitled, wish to apply for protection visas, and would wish to leave the ship and enter Australia. The rescuees have no access to communications with persons off the ship and persons off the ship are unable to communicate with them (Victorian Civil Liberties Council Incorporated v Minister, 2001:para 35).

Federal Court Justice Tony North ruled that the refugees had been illegally detained. In his judgment, the Government had determined 'at the highest level' to 'use an unlawful process to detain and expel the rescuees'. It had breached one of the most basic legal principles, dating back hundreds of years, that no person, whether a citizen or non-citizen, can be held in detention arbitrarily. In granting a writ of habeas corpus for the immediate release of the refugees, he declared: 'An ancient power of the Court is to protect people against detention without lawful authority' (ibid, para 19).

The judge cited a previous High Court judgment, declaring that to allow a government to detain people without trial or clear statutory power would undermine 'the very fabric of freedom under the law' and represent 'tyranny' (Chu Kheng Lim v Minister, 1992:19).

Despite this ruling, the Government continued on its course, having obtained an agreement from the lawyers challenging its actions that it would return the rescuees to Australia if it lost an appeal to the Full Federal Court. The refugees were shipped thousands of kilometres away to Nauru. En route, the Government crammed 237 more refugees, seized off Ashmore Reef, onto the *Manoora*.

In the Full Federal Court, Chief Justice Michael Black upheld Justice North's ruling. However, two judges, Robert French and Bryan Beaumont, held that the Government's actions were authorised by section 61 of the Constitution, which invests the government with executive power, including the socalled prerogative powers formerly exercised by the British monarchy (Ruddock v Vadarlis, 2001).

To find judicial support for the forced expulsion of aliens, the majority reached back to the period of the infamous 'White Australia' policy. Somewhat ironically, they cited the 1891 case of Musgrove v Toy, in which the British Privy Council endorsed a decision by the Victorian Supreme Court involving the exclusion of a Chinese man who had arrived in the port of Melbourne aboard the SS Afghan. The very use of this precedent suggests that the White Australia policy, or at least the nationalist and exclusivist outlook underpinning it, is far from dead.

On 27 November 2001, the High Court brought the *Tampa* case to an abrupt halt (Vadarlis v Minister, 2001). A panel of three justices refused to consider an appeal from the Full Federal Court despite the undeniable existence of 'questions of law' of 'public importance'. In a one-page judgment, they declared that the claim for a writ of habeas corpus had been 'overtaken by events,' namely the Government's forced transfer of the *Tampa* refugees to Nauru.

As a matter of fact, the Government had undertaken to bring the refugees back to Australia should it lose the appeal. Instead, it presented the High Court with a fait accompli, arguing that Australia was no longer detaining the refugees, because they had been removed to Nauru. In effect, the three High Court judges rewarded the Government for thumbing its nose at the legal process.

By the time the case reached the High Court, the Government, supported by the Labor Party, had pushed through parliament a package of legislation retrospectively authorising its conduct and giving military officers wide-ranging authority to board, search, detain and turn around refugee boats, using whatever means are considered 'necessary and reasonable,' including force.

The legislation does not define 'necessary and reasonable force' but even if it did, the definition would seem to be academic because all conduct under the legislation is protected from legal challenge. One section states: 'All action to which this Part applies is taken for all purposes to have been lawful when it occurred.' Another specifies that no legal proceedings can be commenced or continued against the Commonwealth in relation to such action.

These provisions could allow refugees to be brutally treated or their boats to be sunk deliberately to prevent them landing on Australian soil. This is not far-fetched. Shots have already been fired in the direction of at least one over-crowded and sinking boat, whose occupants, Government ministers then falsely accused of throwing children overboard (Head, 2001). And Prime Minister Howard has defended the use of capsicum gas and possibly electric prods by Australian military personnel to force asylum seekers to sail back to Indonesia in an unseaworthy boat that was later shipwrecked off West Timor (Sydney Morning Herald, 2002).

Other precedents established by the post*Tampa* legislation include:
- creation of excision zones where Australian migration law does not apply to parts of the country;
- denial of basic legal rights, including the right to seek legal advice, to detainees held in the excision zones or in Nauru or PNG;
- narrowing of the definition of refugee, particularly by overturning aspects of the High Court's interpretation of the Refugee Convention's requirement for asylum seekers to fear 'persecution';
- allowing immigration officials to draw adverse implications from an asylum seeker's lack of official identity documents;
- banning class and representative actions in refugee cases; imposition of severe jail terms of up to 10 years for escaping or aiding an escape from detention; and
- insertion of a sweeping ouster or 'privative' clause in the Migration Act to attempt to block all judicial review of refugee and immigration decisions made by the government's tribunals.

Even though the latter provision stops short of seeking to override the constitutionally entrenched jurisdiction of the High Court, aspects of this barrage of legislation may be unconstitutional, including on the grounds that they block the exercise of federal judicial power. Nevertheless, the High Court declined to test the validity of the Government's actions and legislation in the *Tampa* case.

Taken together, these measures constitute a decisive strengthening of the power of the executive government and its state apparatus, at the expense of refugees and other noncitizens. As the political discussion surrounding the case indicated, the stripping of legal and democratic rights from stateless individuals, the most defenceless members of society, has wider implications for legally challenging arbitrary or unlawful exercises of government power.

The Political Climate

As the courts deliberated in the *Tampa* case, Government leaders and media commentators applied intense pressure to the judges, arguing that the terrorist attacks in the United States on 11 September 2001 made it essential for the government to wield greater powers. Defence Minister Peter Reith insisted that if Justice North's ruling stood, it would open the floodgates for terrorists to enter the country on refugee boats (O'Loughlin & Skehan, 2001). Without offering a skerrick of evidence, a junior minister, Peter Slipper, claimed there was 'an undeniable linkage between illegals and terrorists' (Sydney Morning Herald, 18/08/01).

Media proprietors and columnists openly called into question the right of courts to test the validity of legislation. An editorial in Sydney's Daily Telegraph attacked Vadarlis and the Victorian Civil Liberties Council for showing 'suspect' judgment. 'The broader issue is the right of a court to act against the wishes of the elected government,' it insisted (Duffy, 2001:23). Sydney Morning Herald columnist Padraic McGuinness labelled the Civil Liberties Council, 'the Council for Criminal Liberties' and expressed the hope that the terror attacks in America would render legal rulings redundant. 'Popular feeling will now ensure that the government will have little difficulty in tightening up on refugee policy so as to diminish the interference of the courts' (McGuinness, 2001:24).

Writing in the Australian, two Australian National University legal academics, Robin Creyke and John McMillan, asserted that the Full Federal Court should have declined to hear the *Tampa* case on the ground that it was non-justiciable (Creyke & McMillan, 2001). The authors went so far as to describe judicial review as a 'negative disruptive factor' (p. 13). Apart from flying in the face of legal authority, this extraordinary argument has a chilling logic. It suggests that governments should be free to defy the law, without the threat of legal challenge, at least in the politically sensitive areas of so-called 'national security' and 'border protection'.

After the Full Federal Court decision was handed down, the Government tried to bully the lawyers who had acted pro bono in arguing the refugees' case. It threatened to pursue them for crippling legal costs if they appealed to the High Court, breaching a longstanding convention of not seeking costs in cases of public importance. It also warned that the lawyers could be charged personally with the expense of keeping the refugees aboard the *Manoora* while the High Court deliberated (Secombe & Marr, 2001).

This intimidatory atmosphere continued throughout the 2001 election campaign, which was entirely dominated by a bipartisan unity between the Liberal-National Party Coalition and the official Labor Party opposition on repelling refugee boats and preventing access to the courts by asylum seekers, as well as other visa applicants.

Global Refugee System in Crisis

The fate of the *Tampa* asylum seekers highlights a grave crisis facing the existing refugee system worldwide. According to the available statistics, the flight of people from their countries of birth grew dramatically in the final two decades of the 20th Century and this mass movement is likely to grow in the 21st (Castles & Miller, 1993:5-8). Increasingly, they are resorting to unauthorised methods of entry, often at great risk to their lives.

Despite implementing draconian measures, governments are having considerable difficulties, logistically, diplomatically and politically, in removing those denied refugee status (van Kessel, 2001:11). Governments are spending massive sums on detecting and detaining unwanted arrivals, deciding their fate and administering the outcomes, while giving decreasing funds to the United Nations High Commissioner for Refugees (UNHCR) 2000, which is responsible for most of the world's displaced persons (Telford, 2001). Canberra spends as much each year on the Refugee Review Tribunal, just one level of the determination process, as it allocates to the UNHCR (ibid, p. 4). Treasurer Peter Costello has confirmed that the misnamed 'Pacific Solution' will cost half a billion dollars in 2001–2002 (Crock & Saul 2002:81).

Over the past two decades, successive Australian governments have taken the policy of seeking to block and deter unwanted arrivals to its logical end by compulsorily detaining asylum seekers, usually in remote, inhospitable semi-desert locations, and, since August 2001, by militarily barring entry to refugees. Severe police and security methods, including the use of mass arrests, water cannon, tear gas and solitary confinement, have failed to quell the unrest in the camps— expressed in hunger strikes, mass breakouts anddetermined protests (Mares, 2001; Australian Broadcasting Corporation, 2001).

How the Refugee Numbers have Grown

In 1951, when the UNHCR was established, there were an estimated 1.5 million refugees worldwide (McMaster, 2001:9). Fifty years later, on January 1, 2000, the UNHCR considered 22.3 million people to be 'of concern'. They included 11.7 million refugees, 1.2 million asylum seekers, 2.5 million repatriated refugees and 6.9 million internally displaced persons and others of concern (UNHCR, 2000:6). Another 13-18 million internally displaced persons were outside the UNHCR's jurisdiction, as were an estimated 3.5 million Palestinians. This gives a total of 43 million.

The number of people 'of concern' to the UNHCR nearly doubled during the 1990s, from 14.9 million in 1990, reaching an all-time high of 27 million in 1995 — in the wake of the Gulf War against Iraq, the fomenting of communalism in Yugoslavia, and the eruption of ethnic warfare in Rwanda and Africa's Great Lakes region (ibid, p. 5).

The rise in refugee numbers has been related to definite economic and political processes, particularly the collapse of the Stalinist-ruled states in Eastern Europe from the late 1980s, the US-led bombing of Iraq, Serbia and Afghanistan and the outbreak of regional conflicts in Eastern Europe, the Middle East, Asia and Africa (Nygh, 2000:2).

More fundamental driving forces are also at work. The increased demand for asylum has occurred amid an unprecedented globalisation of the world economy since the mid-1980s, creating massive flows of international capital, the rapid shift of production processes from country to country and a worldwide labour market (International Committee of the Fourth International, 1999; Castles & Miller, 1993). At the same time, the ever-widening gulf between the capital-rich, technologically advanced and militarily powerful countries and the rest of the world has fuelled the demand for the right to escape poverty (Zolberg, 1992-93).

According to the 1998 United Nations Human Development Report, the three richest people in the world have assets exceeding the combined Gross Domestic Product of the 48 least developed countries, the 15 richest people have assets worth more than the total GDP of sub-Saharan Africa and the 32 richest more assets than the GDP of South Asia. The wealth of the richest 84 individuals exceeds the GDP of China with its 1.2 billion inhabitants.

Of the 4.4 billion people in so-called developing countries, almost three fifths lack basic sanitation, one third have no safe drinking water and one quarter have inadequate housing, while one fifth are undernourished, and the same proportion have no access to decent health services. According to the UN, out of the 147 countries defined as 'developing' some 100 had experienced 'serious economic decline' over the past 30 years (UN, 1998).

Australian Policy: Refugees Demonised

As many commentators have pointed out, Australia experiences only a trickle of the worldwide movement of displaced people (Crock & Saul, 2002). Yet, successive governments have sought to poison public opinion against asylum seekers, leading the Western world in imposing mandatory detention in the early 1990s and now military exclusion in the new century.

The official condemnation of queue jumping is cynical. Far from waiting in an orderly queue, those seeking safe haven in Australia confront impossible situations, terrible delays and obvious discrimination. Those likely to be the most needy — refugees in Africa, Asia and the Middle East — are the least likely to be accepted.

Out of the 7,500 places for offshore applicants in 2000, 45 percent were given to Europeans, leaving 2,206 places for the entire Middle East and 1,738 for all of Africa. The Australian High Commission in Nairobi (covering 34 African countries, including the Horn of Africa) had 8,000 applicants for asylum in September 1999, with a further 2,000 to be registered. There was an even greater backlog in Islamabad, which covers Iran and Afghanistan, as well as Pakistan (Mares, 2001:20).

Moreover, the Australian government cuts its miserable 12,000-a-year quota of humanitarian and protection visas for offshore applicants by the number of asylum seekers who reach Australia independently and are granted refugee status. This policy pits the two groups — both in urgent need of protection — against each other.

Labelling asylum seekers who arrive without permission as illegal entrants is equally misleading. In most cases they have broken no laws, and certainly have not been convicted of any offence. In any event, because refugees, by necessity, are often forced to escape from their countries and mislead authorities, Article 31 of the Refugee Convention stipulates that governments should not penalise applicants 'on account of illegal entry or presence'. This provision also forbids 'practices that might deter refugees from seeking protection' and requires contracting states 'to treat all refugees alike' whether or not they have some other lawful reason for being in the territory (Esmaeili & Wells, 2000:229). The Australian Government is clearly in breach of these responsibilities. Its policy is not only punitive, but also designed to deter asylum seekers.

It is hardly surprising that human rights groups, refugee advocacy groups and the United Nations have criticised the Australian Government's unprecedented response to the *Tampa* asylum seekers. Amnesty International has condemned the Australian Government, saying the action taken was 'a flagrant violation of the 1951 UN Refugee Convention to which Australia is a state party' (Amnesty International, 2001).

However, the *Tampa* affair also exposes the underlying weakness of the Refugee Convention. The fact is that the Convention, even augmented by other treaties, does not impose a positive obligation on signatory states to accept refugees. The Howard Government can argue that its 'Pacific Solution' is perfectly legitimate under the Convention.

The Convention's Fundamental Flaws

It has long been recognised that the Refugee Convention is extremely narrow and does not assist the vast majority of the displaced persons. As noted a decade ago by Hathaway:

> Most Third World refugees remain de facto excluded, as their flight
> is more often prompted by natural disaster, war, or broadly based

political and economic turmoil than by 'persecution,' at least as that term is understood in the Western context (Hathaway, 1990:10 11).

The Convention is deficient in at least four primary respects (Hathaway, 1990:611; Nygh, 2000:3-7).

In the first place: it does not protect the starving, the destitute, those fleeing war and civil war or even natural disaster, let alone those seeking to escape economic oppression. Its narrow focus on individuals who are persecuted does not allow for mass exoduses in the face of suffering, injustice or discrimination that is not considered serious enough to amount to persecution.

Its requirement that this persecution be on the specific grounds of race, nationality, religious belief, political opinion or membership of a particular social group, does not apply to people seeking refuge from torture, cruel punishment or other infringements of democratic rights, no matter how serious, inflicted for other reasons, despite efforts to extend the interpretation of 'particular social group' to include gender, sexual preference and childbearing (Applicant A v Minister, 1997).

Secondly: the Convention does not create a right to enter another state, only a limited obligation on a national state not to expel or return a refugee to a state where he or she faces persecution. In fact, the Convention does not recognise the individual's right to asylum, only the right of national states to decide who enters their territory. As recently stated in the Australian High Court:

> The right of asylum is a right of States, not of the individual: no individual, including those seeking asylum, may assert a right to enter the territory of a State of which that individual is not a national (Gummow in Minister v Ibrahim, 2000).

Thirdly: even those accepted as refugees have no right to permanent residence and hence can be consigned to a tenuous and insecure status. The principle of non-refoulement under the Convention's Article 33(1) allows them to be removed to a so-called safe third country or to be forcibly repatriated to their home country once a government considers that the reasons for refugee status have ceased, as provided in Article 1C(5).

Fourthly: the Convention only assists asylum seekers who manage, invariably by means designated as 'illegal,' to arrive physically in the country where they seek refuge. It does not impose any obligation on a country to take offshore applicants, that is, the overwhelming majority of people languishing in refugee camps throughout the poorest parts of the world, whether in their own countries or neighbouring states.

This fact further exposes the hypocrisy of governments that blackguard unwanted arrivals as 'queue jumpers', 'illegals' and 'forum shoppers'. Refugees can only obtain the limited protection available under the Convention by escaping and entering a 'safe' country without permission.

Cold War Origins

These fundamental flaws reflect the Convention's Cold War origins. It was drawn up in the aftermath of the Second World War and the Nazi Holocaust, which had caused the displacement of more than 40 million people within Europe. The knowledge that the advanced capitalist countries had refused to open their borders to many fleeing fascist persecution led to a broadly held sentiment that never again should refugees be turned away.

These democratic aspirations were incorporated in the Convention, which set out that all asylum-seekers— defined as those having a well-founded fear of persecution — were to be guaranteed certain inalienable rights, specifically that of refuge. Nevertheless, key governments only accepted the Convention on the basis that it did not create any duty to grant permanent residence and that they retained the sovereign right to decide which refugees ought to be allowed entry to their countries (Hathaway, 1999:2).

Those who framed the Convention were also mindful of broader political considerations. In upholding the right to political asylum, the West sought to strengthen its democratic credentials against the Soviet Union and Eastern bloc countries and specifically to hold the door open for political dissidents from the Stalinist regimes. The very conception of 'persecution' was tailored to give Western governments, ideological kudos for providing sanctuary to 'defectors' to the 'free world' (Collinson, 1993).

These political origins have been acknowledged judicially. Thus, one Australian High Court judge has emphasised that the participating governments 'had no commitment to basing the Convention in the international promotion of human rights' (Gummow in Minister v Ibrahim, 2000).

With the collapse of the Soviet Union and Eastern European states, the major powers felt themselves to have been 'liberated' from the democratic restraints imposed in an earlier period. Once the Cold War imperatives no longer applied, Western governments began to declare that the Convention was too wide.

In the words of one senior UNHCR official:

> Broadly speaking, two parallel trends have emerged, both of which have impacted negatively on the accessibility of asylum and the quality of treatment received by refugees and asylum seekers. The first has been the growth in an overly restrictive application of the 1951 Refugee Convention and its 1967 Protocol, coupled with a formidable range of obstacles erected by states to prevent legal and physical access to their territory. The second is the bewildering proliferation of alternative protection regimes of more limited duration and guaranteeing lesser rights than those contained in the 1951 Convention (Feller, 2001:7).

The Need for an Alternative Perspective

Many claims are made that these trends reflect public opinion. For now, let me merely suggest that governments go to such lengths as falsely claiming that refugees threw children overboard in order to manipulate and distort public opinion.

For a genuine appraisal of democratic opinion, a viable alternative perspective must be advanced, one that corresponds to the requirements of global economic and social life and the needs and aspirations of the vast majority of the world's people, rather than the vested interests of government leaders and corporate elites.

A number of authors have suggested possible models for replacing the Refugee Convention with new international frameworks for protecting and assisting refugees, usually with a wider definition of refugee status (Arulanantham, 2000; Schuck, 1997; Freedman, 1995; Hathaway, 1990; Burton, 1988). None of these models, however, challenge the underlying assumption that nation-states and national borders will continue to exist throughout the 21st Century.

Instead, they seek ways to dilute the refugee obligations of nation-states according to what the authors consider politically palatable. Hathaway has argued specifically for tailoring proposals for change to meet the needs of national governments:

> In an international legal system based on the self-interest of states, it is critical that principled reform proceed in a manner which anticipates and responds to the needs of governments ... [with

117

support for a] broader [if shallower] level of protection for most of the world's refugees' (Hathaway, 1997: page number).

In general, these authors invoke notions such as limited safe havens, temporary protection, international, regional and bilateral cooperation and burden sharing. They also seek to arbitrarily wall off the refugee regime from migration programs, arguing that this will ease public concern over so-called asylum-driven migration and people smuggling.

Aside from leaving refugee policy in the hands of national governments, this approach is based on maintaining the strict distinction between refugees and migrants. In a global world, and one increasingly dominated by social inequality, this is a spurious, misleading and ultimately unreal perspective. As a senior Canadian immigration official has acknowledged:

> Almost all parts of the world are witnessing major migratory movements. While in 1965, 65 million people were living long term outside their countries of normal residence, by 1990 there were 130 million and in 2000 an estimated 150 million. Some are persons with legal status in their adopted countries. Most are in an irregular situation and try by various means to regularise their status (van Kessel, 2001:10).

This demand for a more decent life will only grow amid ever-wider disparities in wealth and life opportunities. Moreover, the advent of new forms of mass information, information technology and greater accessibility to air travel will accelerate and facilitate the movement of large numbers of politically and economically oppressed people.

Citizenship and Democratic Rights

There is a profound connection between democratic rights and the rights of the most vulnerable in society — those denied entry to, or citizenship of, a country where they feel secure and able to participate meaningfully in political life.

Without the right to live securely with full political and social rights, democracy itself is meaningless. How can any basic democratic right, such as free speech, freedom of association and individual liberty, be exercised if a citizen is not free to leave a country and enter another? Does not genuine democracy require an absolute right to escape from intolerable political, economic or social oppression?

As one study noted, in the 20th century:

The possession of a nationality became a matter of crucial, practical importance to the individual. The stateless person has no right of residence in any territory, no right to apply for employment or establish a business in any particular place. In some countries, a stateless person has only limited access to the legal system and its protection. One needs a nationality in order to enjoy basic security of residence somewhere (Dummett & Nicol, 1991:13).

Of course, the argument for a right to free movement has deep-going implications. It fundamentally challenges the prevailing conception that national sovereignty is paramount. Yet, it is important to recognise that the existence of nation-states, partitioning the globe into a patchwork of larger and smaller entities each with their own border controls and exclusion regimes, is not natural or of ancient origin. Modern nationalism and general restrictions on the movement of people emerged only in the late 19th and early 20th centuries. Dummett and Nicol have pointed out that:

> In earlier periods, restriction was by no means unknown but it was neither so general nor so systematic … Before the 1914 war, it was possible to travel between a number of countries without a passport, and with no restriction on taking work after arrival. With the price of a passage, an individual could take a free decision to look abroad for a new life; even without it, one could 'run away to sea', work a passage and try one country after another (ibid, pp. 11-12).

As an example, the authors quote Robert Louis Stevenson's account of his own unhindered voyage to America, published as The Amateur Emigrant (1895).

From the late 19th century, however, border restrictions began to limit these movements.

> Instead of being 'chained to the soil' of a feudal lord, the twentieth century poor gradually became chained to the territory of their countries of origin because other countries' rules forbade them entry (ibid, p. 13).

The new shackling of the poor is bound up with the division of the planet into a minority of wealthy, exploiting nations on the one hand and a majority of colonial or semi-colonial states on the other, producing a social polarisation that, as the statistics I cited earlier indicate, has grown to unbearable proportions. The rights of the poor and oppressed can therefore be defended only as part of a wider struggle against the current socio-economic order.

Ultimately, meaningful democracy cannot be separated from social equality. How can there be genuine democratic participation and control over society if a small minority of the world's population monopolises the wealth and, moreover, can block the poor from fleeing destitution or persecution? I suggest that both democracy and social equality demand the right of all people to move wherever they wish around the world; the right to live, work and study wherever they choose, enjoying the political, civil and social rights and benefits available to all. Various commentators, while acknowledging the problems of the nation-state system and its inability to deliver the democratic potential of globalised information technology, have dismissed this conception as utopian (for example, Davidson, 1997).

Nevertheless, some attempts have been made to elaborate such a new paradigm. In their recent work, Empire, Hardt and Negri (2000) argued that the power of transnational corporations and new forms of labour and production have already created a new imperial global order. They identified new conceptions of identity and difference, networks of communication and control, and paths of migration, contending that they establish the basis for a truly democratic global society without national state borders. This is not the place to discuss the flaws in their analysis, but the very fact that their volume has attracted a wide international readership demonstrates an emerging recognition of the need for a global reshaping of human civilisation.

The realisation of a truly global perspective of liberating humanity from national straitjackets will require reorganising society completely along democratic, egalitarian and fraternal lines. Why not make that a goal for the 21st century? The alternative is to leave the vast majority of refugees and displaced persons denied protection.

REFERENCES

Channel 9 (2001), A Current Affair interview with Prime Minister John Howard by Mike Munro, 28 Aug 2001,
   http://www.pm.gov.au/news/interviews/2001/interview1190.htm
Arulanantham, A. T. (2000), 'Restructured safe havens: A proposal for reform of the refugee protection system', *Human Rights Quarterly*, 22(1), 156.
Amnesty International Australia (2001), 'Amnesty international calls for Urgent Action against Australia', 30 Aug 2001 http://www.amnesty.org.au/news/tampa30Aug2001-press.html (accessed 3 October 2001).
Applicant A v Minister for Immigration and Ethnic Affairs (1997) 190 CLR 225.

Australian Broadcasting Corporation (2001), 'The Inside Story', Four Corners report, 13 Aug 2001, http://www.abc.net.au/4corners/stories/s344246.htm (accessed 14 August 2001).

Burton, E. (1988), 'Leasing rights: a new international instrument for protecting refugees and compensating host countries', 19 Columbia Human Rights Law Review.

Castles, S. & Miller, M. (1993), *The Age of Migration: International Population Movement in the Modern World.* Macmillan: London.

Chu Kheng Lim v Minister for Immigration, Local Government and Ethnic Affairs (1992) 176 CLR 1.

Collinson, S. (1993), Beyo*nd Borders: West European Migration Policy Towards the 21st Century.* Royal Institute of International Affairs: London.

Creyke, R. & McMillan, J. (2001), 'No place for dispute in court', *The Australian*, 25 Sept 2001, p. 13.

Crock, M. & Saul, B. (2002), *Future Seekers: Refugees and the Law in Australia.* The Federation Press: Sydney.

Commonwealth of Australia, Migration Act 1958.

Davidson, A. (1997), 'Globalism, the Regional Citizen and Democracy', in B. Galligan & C. Sampford, *Rethinking Human Rights.* The Federation Press: Sydney.

Duffy, M. (2001), 'Outraged elite all at sea', Daily Telegraph, 8 Sept 2001, p. 23.

Dummett, A. & Nicol, A. (1991), *Subjects, Citizens, Aliens and Others, Nationality and Immigration Law.* Weidenfeld and Nicholson: London.

Esmaeili, H. & Wells, B. (2000), 'The Temporary' Refugees: Australia's Legal Response to the Arrival of Iraqi and Afghan Boatpeople', *UNSW Law Journal*, 23(3), 224 245.

Feller, E. (2001), 'The Convention at 50: the way ahead for refugee protection', Forced Migration Review, 10, 6.

Freedman, P. (1995), 'International intervention to combat the explosion of refugees and internally displaced persons', *Georgetown Immigration Law Journal*, 9(3), page number.

Hardt, M. & Negri, A. (2000), Empire. Harvard University Press: Cambridge.

Hathaway, J. (1990), 'A reconsideration of the underlying premise of refugee law' *Harvard International Law Journal*, 31(1), 166183.

Hathaway, J. (1997), 'Can International Refugee Law be Made Relevant Again?' in J. Hathaway (Ed.), *Reconceiving International Refugee Law.* Martinus Nijhoff Publishers: The Hague.

Hathaway, J. (1999), Can International Refugee Law Be Made Relevant Again? World Refugee Information, United States Committee for Refugees http://www.refugees.org/world/articles/intl_law_wrs9 6.html.

Head, M. (2001), 'Australian election: The Howard government's big lie unravels', World Socialist Web Site, 10 Nov 2001, http://www.wsws.org/articles/2001/nov2001/refu n10.shtml (accessed 10 November 2001).

International Committee of the Fourth International (1999), *Globalization and the International Working Class: A Marxist Assessment.* Mehring Books: Sydney.

Mares. P. (2001), *Borderline: Australia's treatment of refugees and asylum seekers.* University of New South Wales Press: Sydney.

Marr, D. (2001), 'Arne Rinnan, a man who's not like us', *Sydney Morning Herald*, 22 Dec 2001, p. 20.

McGuinness, P. (2001), ' Terror's shockwaves echo in the waters of the Pacific ', *Sydney Morning Herald*, 13 Sept 2001, p. 24.

McMaster, D. (2001), *Asylum Seekers: Australia's Response to Refugees.* Melbourne University Press: Melbourne.

Minister for Immigration and Multicultural Affairs v Ibrahim (2000) 175 ALR 585.

Musgrove v Toy [1891] AC 272.

Nygh, P. (2000), 'The Future of the United Nations' 1951 Refugees Convention' [2000] Australian International Law Journal, 124.

O'Loughlin, T. & Skehan, C. (2001), 'Reith blasts court as new boat arrives', *Sydney Morning Herald*, 17 Sept 2001.

Ruddock v Vadarlis [2001] FCA 1329.

Schuck, P. (1997), 'Refugee burdensharing: a modest proposal', *Yale Journal of International Law*, 22(2), 243 297.

Secombe, M. & Marr, D. (2001), 'Appeal and you'll pay: liberties lawyers warned on court costs,' *Sydney Morning Herald*, 18 Sept 2001, p. 6.

Sydney Morning Herald (2001), 'Minister claims link between boatpeople and terrorists', 18 Sept 2001.

Sydney Morning Herald (2002), 'PM backs troops over electric prod claims,' 16 April 2002, http://www.smh.com.au/articles/2002/04/16/1018333497326.html (accessed 16 April 2002).

Telford, J. (2001), 'UNHCR and emergencies: a new role or back to basics?', Forced Migration Review, 1 0, 4245.

United Nations (1998), Human Development Report: Consumption for Human Development, http://hdr.undp.org/reports/global/1998/en/

UNHCR (2000), Refugees by Numbers. Vadarlis v Minister for Immigration and Multicultural Affairs and Ors M93/2001 at http://www.austlii.edu.au/au/other/hca/transcripts/2001/M93/2.html (accessed 30 November 2001).

van Kessel, G. (2001), 'Global migration and asylum', Forced Migration Review, 10, 10-13.

Victorian Civil Liberties Council Incorporated v Minister for Immigration and Multicultural Affairs [2001] FCA 1297.

Zolberg, A. (19921993), 'International Migrants and Refugees in Historical Perspective', Refugees, 16.

CHAPTER EIGHT

WHO ARE 'WE'?

INCLUSION AND EXCLUSION IN AUSTRALIAN POLITICAL DISCOURSE

MICHAEL DARCY AND NATALIE BOLZAN

> "We decide who will come to Australia, and the circumstances in which they come!"

Prime Minister John Howard's rather clumsy campaign slogan rang out so loudly and so often from television sets and posters across Australia during the 2001 Federal election campaign that no one who was in the country in those weeks could have missed its significance. These words summed up a raft of controversial policy decisions and legislation enacted by the Australian Government in previous months, particularly arising from the 'Tampa incident', which is described in previous chapters. The Tampa, however, merely provided an opportunity for the Government to crystallise its rhetoric on the issue of asylum seekers - and in so doing - to secure wide political support for long standing policies designed to discourage, exclude and reject certain people making their own way to Australia (outside of official bureaucratic channels) to seek protection and a better life.

In this chapter we argue that these words, and the political strategy they exemplify, are at least as significant for their impact on the meaning of being 'Australian', and how to be Australian, as they are for the asylum seekers and refugees themselves. The words were chosen carefully, not for the ears of the so-called boat people, but for those already enjoying residence in Australia and membership of the Australian community. The impact of these words has extended beyond the life of the so-called crisis to ongoing definitions of what it means to be Australian. "We decide" projected a compelling sense of empowerment to those about to cast their votes: a sense that 'we' could determine our future by consensual and collective means, and that the alternative - not to take this power - was to surrender Australia to chaotic forces of global population growth and supra national institutions. The 'we' of Howard's slogan invokes strongly communitarian ideas of participation and of shared values and interests. 'We' places the speaker and the listener together in the subject position in relation to the active voiced verb 'decide'. 'We' is inclusive by virtue of the fact that it is also exclusive – 'we' calls up the comfortable dualism by which we can define ourselves entirely in relation to what we are not: the object, 'them'.

Since the gold rushes of the mid nineteenth century, debates about immigration in Australia have, not surprisingly, often turned on constructions of 'difference'. Only latterly have Australians turned away from historic insistence on the mythical 'White Australia' to realise the economic and social benefits of welcoming skilled and unskilled labour regardless of source. Popular support for the 25 year old official policy of multi-culturalism has always been tenuous, especially amongst those living in the most homogenously Anglo-Irish communities. This is clearly evidenced by the pattern of support for Pauline Hanson's One Nation in elections around the turn of the century. Nonetheless, the experience of observing the horrors of apartheid South Africa and hearing the stories of the 'stolen generation' of indigenous Australians, amongst other things, have lent weight to the more dominant (and usually more highly educated) voices of the urban middle class, leading to the valorisation in dominant and official discourse of themes rejecting racism and discrimination. For a time the dominant construction of the Australian 'we' was actively being broadened as, through formal education and the popular media, 'we' acknowledged 'our' diversity and confronted 'our' cultural and inter-cultural histories. Without race or even common culture as its defining feature, Australians appeared ready to embrace the challenge of defining themselves by their very diversity and tolerance.

Where democracy is constrained within geographic borders, however, this may well be a greater challenge than it first appeared. To understand the lasting effects on the Australian identity of the "we" of Prime Minister Howard's rhetoric - to discover and understand the nature of the Australian community he sought to invoke - we need to understand exactly how this discursive construction of Australia has been sustained and its long-term cultural impacts.

Well before the Tampa and the 2001 election campaign the Australian Government were using asylum seekers as part of a deliberate discursive strategy, constructing an identity for Australia and Australians which was inward looking and exclusive. Almost a year earlier, then Immigration Minister Philip Ruddock was criticised by the Refugee Council of Australia for distributing an information kit to the Middle Eastern media "replete with a... video showing Australia bedeviled by man eating sharks and deadly snakes" (Orphant, 2001). Of course, few Australian residents ever confront such dangers and the campaign is likely to have had minimal effect in war-torn Afghanistan, but in Australia it clearly patronised asylum seekers as simple people who could be easily frightened and minimised the potential dangers that refugees might already be facing. More significant was the threat from the human denizens of Australia described in the Government's draft pamphlet: "...illegal arrivals are often the subject of racial hatred and violence as citizens are angry at having to support them" (Taylor, 2001). Indeed the clear implication was to reverse the presumption that 'boat people' were refugees and to install the notion that they are assumed to be 'illegals' until they could prove otherwise. 'Illegals' in this context means they freely chose to take the risks they did, not to survive, but to circumvent immigration processes and in politico-bureaucratic language, 'achieve a migration outcome'. Tangled up in this discursive shift was the related notion that the existing Australian population (described worthily as 'citizens') could be expected to respond with hateful but righteous resentment.

The particular phrase 'achieve a migration outcome' was used extensively in the public utterances of immigration officials in Australia. This neatly bureaucratic term focused attention on the supposed overriding desirability of ultimately living in Australia as opposed to the fear and poverty that asylum seekers were trying to leave behind. It stands in strange contrast to the land of dangerous animals and resentful racists presented to potential refugees by the Australian Government in their countries of origin. The very notion that Australia is so desirable a place that people would risk their lives to achieve a 'migration outcome' tells Australians that they should also do what they can to preserve what they have.

In this construction, not only is Australia a desirable destination but the character and values of its citizenry are also valuable and susceptible to destruction if 'undesirables' are allowed to settle here. This contradiction can only be sustained by a deep and irrational sense of self-satisfaction coupled with deliberately induced fear. As van Dijk (1987) noted, discourse is not just a symptom or sign of the presence of racism, but rather it essentially constructs, reproduces and transmits the racist beliefs and actions of the White majority.

After the Tampa, the Government, with the enthusiastic support of the tabloid media, embarked on a renewed and more vigorous discursive strategy of demonisation and dehumanisation of asylum seekers while at the same time encouraging Australian self-congratulation. While asylum seekers still sat on the deck of the container vessel, the Prime Minister began the process with the charge that "they are trying to intimidate us with our own decency" (Clennell & Crichton, 2001:1). He dismissed the humanitarian crisis on board, bracketing it with other unauthorised boat arrivals, by saying: "every situation has stories of hunger strikes, even suggestions of throwing children overboard" (op cit).

Of course this last image became a slogan in itself in the heat of the election campaign when, six weeks later, the Howard Government claimed that the refugees did indeed throw children overboard in an attempt to 'intimidate' the government "out of its tough boat people policy by asylum seekers throwing children overboard" (Cornford & Grattan, 2001:1). The fact that by February 2002, after the election and under Opposition scrutiny, some members of the Government were apologising for this claim (Hopkins, 2002) is in some ways a secondary issue. By the time the press had reported the item, asylum seekers had been defined in the public arena as people who would risk the lives of their own children to get what they wanted. This idea was created by the Government and media with no foundation in fact. It nonetheless gained prominence in the public discourse about asylum seekers, demonstrating a clearly orchestrated campaign by the Government to demonise the refugees and to construct them as very different from 'us'.

The Government very carefully and consistently developed the idea of asylum seekers as different from 'us' and more importantly, 'not the sort of people' Australia welcomes (Hopkins, 2002), and no amount of contradictory evidence seemed sufficient to displace the need for people to construct a rhetorical, cultural and physical boundary between 'them' and 'us'. The policy of compulsory detention, often for many months and without regard for individual circumstances, is the physical manifestation of this. Most significantly, however, in accepting a political rhetoric which promised control over the composition of the community, Australians began to redefine themselves in ways which ultimately diminish our capacity to shape our own society.

For example, in popular media and Government statements of the time the people who arrived by boat, seeking asylum in Australia, were consistently referred to as 'queue jumpers' and the Government used, and has never retracted from their position of this depiction, to staunchly defend mandatory detention on the basis that anyone who arrives in Australian territory under their own steam has, at the very least, misbehaved. 'Queue jumpers' are people who do not follow due process; they displace other worthy applicants and disadvantage those who are playing by the rules. 'Queue jumpers' are by definition aggressive, selfish and seek to obtain resources or goods that are rationed and can only be fairly distributed by reference to position on an orderly queue - but what does this say about Australians?

This construction serves to distance previous immigrants, who have come to Australia as either refugees or via any other immigration process, from contemporary asylum seekers. People living in Australia who endured a long wait whilst their immigration application was processed, who remained in refugee camps on 'the queue' can now turn to the boat people and identify them as different, as 'not like me'. In a country where a quarter of the population are overseas born, the importance of creating a division between those who have previously migrated to Australia from hostile and war torn homelands and these recent refugees should not be underestimated. It would be hard for previous migrants to conclude that later arrivals should not be allowed asylum, but to say that these refugees are not acceptable because of their behaviour and lack of respect for due process, creates a 'worthy' refugee and the 'others'. Just as Robbin (2000) argues categories of "race" and "ethnicity" have multiple connotations that evoke dilemmas and contradictions about self, group membership, community and governance, so do descriptions of people clearly establish who it is that we are in contrast to who it is that they are. Of course the counterpoint image here is one of Australians as patient queuers and compliant rule-followers, which stands in salient contrast to the popular self-image of self-reliant 'larrikin' individualists who came to Australia as adventurers if not convicts.

The behaviour of asylum seekers whilst in detention also received massive media and Government attention. Episodes of violence and self-harm are offered as further convincing evidence that the detainees have

127

different and unacceptable values and codes of behaviour which make them unsuitable to join the Australian 'we'. This depiction is rarely contextualised with information regarding conditions in the detention facilities or lengthy processing periods, but is framed in terms of an ungrateful group who are not protesting their conditions but rioting. Furthermore they were described as not only destroying the property in the detention centre, but as cruelly sewing together their lips and, even more confrontingly, those of the children in detention to gain sympathy (*Sydney Morning Herald,* 21/01/02; BBC News, 20/01/02). Quite clearly these refugees were behaving in ways which were terrifyingly different and possibly even sub-human.

Protest itself has thus been constructed as 'un-Australian', unless it falls within government and media defined limits, as a sign of ingratitude and failure to appreciate how 'lucky' they are to be here, something of which 'we' Australians supposedly would never be guilty.

The transmutation of the people coming to Australia by boat occurred as they moved from asylum seekers to refugees to illegal non-immigrants. With this changing construction comes a shift in seeing these people as a group in need, a group who sought the compassion and help of Australians, to a group of people who were trying to cheat the system, manipulate a country and threaten those values and beliefs which Australians held dear. Evidence that this construction has taken hold is plentiful, especially in the context of latter day security scares related to international terrorism and the war in Iraq.

In clarifying the plight of those people who seek asylum, Australians could extend a hand, offer solace and perpetuate a belief in ourselves as generous and willing to share some of our good fortune in living in a peaceful country with those less fortunate. By reconstructing the asylum seekers as queue jumpers with no respect for either property or person and, even worse, no real care for their children, Australians are able to shut the gate and say 'fend for yourself, you are not welcome in this country, we will not be manipulated, we have the right to protect our borders'.

The effect of these strategies is to revive a form of Australian nationalism and an Australian identity which is not explicitly focused on the historical values of race and cultural difference, but on the perception of different standards of behaviour: Australians are people who would not 'jump the queue', 'throw children overboard' or 'riot'. Anyone who does these things could never be Australian, regardless of the circumstances in which these things occurred. Of course, this line of thinking is unsustainable if the desperate actions of asylum seekers are put into human context, thus the need for dehumanising and objectifying the individuals concerned. 'Standards of behaviour' becomes a proxy for race and cultural difference. Xenophobia is a fear of things we do not understand and the actions of asylum seekers are not understandable because they are not contextualised, their human stories are rarely told.

Nationalism and fear of outsiders has new significance across the post September 11th western world. Of course the coincidence in time of the attacks on New York and Washington and a wave of Middle Eastern asylum seekers reaching Australia was no coincidence at all, but the immediate reaction of Government officials in Australia was to construct the refugee boats not as a symptom of the terror in Afghanistan, but as a conduit for Afghani terrorists to infiltrate themselves into Australia. This creative turn in the Government's strategy cynically deployed fear for a political purpose - because some might be dangerous we should trust none of them - which is but a short step in the receptive public mind from saying all Muslims are terrorists. This type of strategy is well known in so-called 'law and order' debates where candidates present themselves as the only ones who will protect an innocent and defenceless public from criminals.

In starting this book we heard the voices of young people who are 'fenced out' by Australia's refugee policy, but to understand the impact of the Government's discursive strategy on Australians, we now turn to the voices of young people who are 'fenced in' by these policies. The following provides an insight into the way in which the images presented in the media are reflected in the sentiments of young Australians and also suggests the emergence of resistant readings of the dominant discourse. The responses also show a much more textured understanding of the situation than is reflected in current refugee policy or government rhetoric.

The findings reported here come from research conducted by Badham in 2002, with 51 young people including those who are from non-English speaking and refugee backgrounds, between the ages of 10 and 20 years in rural, regional and urban locations in N.S.W., for Streetwize Communications (unpublished research).

Young people were aware of the power of language to construct an understanding of refugees as people who were acting in ways unacceptable to fair minded Australians by the use in the media of terms such as 'boat people', 'queue jumpers' and 'illegals':

> 'when people say the word 'boat people' it seems negative to me. It seems like they're not wanted here. It seems like they're not people – less than people. They're nothing to us. That's how it describes them to me',

> '"boat people" makes them sound like rejects'.

Not surprisingly the variety of terms used in the media to describe asylum seekers led to some confusion. The term refugee was thought to describe 'people running way from wars', suffering on leaky boats and people seeking to escape hardship or persecution at home, whilst the term asylum seeker was understood to describe people who 'just want to come to Australia' and will do whatever it takes to permanently settle in Australia, a land of great opportunity.

The opportunity within the discourse on refugees to distinguish between legitimate refugees and illegal immigrants also provided a space to distinguish between the current group of refugees and other settled refugees. The discursive strategy of 'othering' offered in the media was used by some young people to distinguish between worthy refugees, such as their families and similar Australians, and unworthy refugees, such as the 'queue jumpers'. People who had themselves migrated to Australia through a humanitarian program distinguished the refugees from themselves by referring to them as 'non-document' holders. Some young people, particularly those from migrant backgrounds, described asylum seekers as delaying the immigration process for people seeking family reunion and other kinds of visas. The vigorous discursive strategy of demonising asylum seekers was evident amongst some of the young people who clearly articulated the negative consequences of these impatient queue jumpers for other potential immigrants to Australia who were obeying the rules:

> 'in my country we have wars and I had to ask to be a refugee. I didn't get to come just like that. I had to wait. They won't'.

The image of refugees as being provided with resources to which they were not entitled was reflected in the understandings of some young people who believed that detention centres provided comfortable accommodation, English lessons, personal items, high-level health care and regular meals to detainees. It was believed that refugees received large welfare handouts from the government and that the objective for some of the asylum seekers was 'getting the dole'. Several young people were critical of the 'ungrateful' behaviour of detainees, based on media reports that depicted these people protesting their conditions or rioting. Such young people did not frame the actions of the detainees in the detention centres as protest against unacceptable living conditions, but as manipulative rioting to obtain more welfare benefits than they were currently enjoying:

> 'they get free food and stuff. I don't reckon they should be here if they aren't going to be grateful'.

The image of asylum seekers as 'queue jumpers' who unfairly access resources and disadvantage those who wait their turn is evident in the understandings of young Australians, but not entirely uncontested. It was seen by some that these people were fleeing for their lives, young Australians' spoke of the hardship endured by these refugees, the fear and persecution they faced in their home-land and the desperation they must have felt in order to undertake the boat journey to Australia:

> 'To put yourself and your family on a boat to try and get here – knowing you might sink before you get here – you wouldn't do it unless you were extremely desperate and its not something you'd give your life savings for unless you really needed help. I think its something we should really be compassionate about. They're people who are escaping atrocities, or terror. They don't do it just because they think 'I'd like to go on boat', they do it because they are probably not going to survive in their own country and when it comes to it, anyone would do that if they wanted to survive'.

Young people offered a challenge to the idea that detention centres provided a cosy refuge demanding 'would Australian's be grateful if they were placed in something like (Woomera)?' They described refugees as having no rights and being locked up 'in the middle of nowhere, with barbed wire, all around (you) nothing but desert'.

Young people articulated a belief in the social construction of a refugee problem rather than the presence of a real problem and the role of the media was seen as central to this. Some of the young people were well aware of the power of the media to deliver a particular message and, in so doing, highjack the debate: 'really, we only see what they want us to see'.

The attacks in the United States on September 11 were seen to have brought about a change in Australia's attitude, 'before that (September 11th) Australians did not care. They didn't notice (refugees)'. For some, this change included the belief that:

'some of them are terrorists. This is why the Australian Government does not want the refugees here. Because some of them are terrorists, they want to do what they did in America'.

For others the change was about the Government's desire to ingratiate ourselves with the United States rather than any real fear of a refugee 'crisis'.

Beyond being critical of the media and government in constructing refugees as unworthy queue jumpers who sought to cheat other immigrants out of their rightful place, some young Australians suggested that the problem lay more with who we, as Australians, are becoming. As one young person noted:

'the major problem we have with the refugees isn't the people coming in. It's the people here. The people are influenced by the government'.

Some identified racism as underpinning the tough Australian stance:

'because they're coming from Arab backgrounds – Iraq, Iran, Africa, and stuff. That's the only reason'.

They described an Australian response which was harsh, selfish and punishing of people who would do what any reasonable person struggling to survive would do. Furthermore they noted the hypocrisy around Australian refugee policy:

'Australia once needed refugees to come and fix up the country and now they don't want them – they just want to get rid of them'.

It is clear that whilst young people from schools around NSW reflected the dominant discourses identified in the media and public comments made by politicians, they were in many cases critical of the construction of asylum seekers as acting in ways which were un-Australian. Furthermore they opened up the debate a little by reflecting on Australian behaviour and suggesting that this may also be un-Australian.

It is now three years since the Tampa rescued and attempted to deliver 433 refugees to Australian shores. The refugee crisis described by the Government has abated and the need for high profile, tough government decisions on who we let in has, in the main, passed. Occasional stories still appear in the media around individual visa decisions and while there are still too many people who remain in immigration detention in Australia, the Government has begun to individualise the treatment of some asylum seekers. By softening their treatment the Government has made concessions in ways that have managed to defuse the arguments of all but most committed fighters

132

around the rights of refugees. In 2004 the Immigration Minister Vanstone stated "Australia has made it clear all along that it will take its fair share of refugees" (Skehan, 2004:6), this 'clear' intention has resulted in a high percentage of refugees who have been detained for more than two and a half years recently being granted refugee status. The Government has found a way to respond to the more urgent criticism of its treatment of asylum seekers but has left unresolved the larger issue of who the real Australians are.

The whole debate initiated by the Howard Government's response to the Tampa refugees has had an impact beyond the lives of the Tampa refugees to influence our basic understandings of what it means to be Australians. A shift has taken place at the most fundamental level of language. How we can talk about ourselves as Australians has narrowed, such that any leadership attempting to challenge the dominant construction runs the risk of being dismissed as out of step with the way the world is. Mark Latham as Federal Opposition Leader demonstrates the current difficulty in discussing who we are when he advises we should catch up with up with the modern reality, and not celebrate diversity for diversity sake (Koutsoukis, 2004:1). What remains for us to celebrate is, however, unclear.

In this new discursive environment of narrowed understanding of what it is to be Australian, we hear a note of resistance in the voice of young people. This cohort who have grown up with, sat in classrooms beside and played sports with people from nearly every nation of earth, have a different understanding of what it means to be Australian. The personal imperative of living in an Australia defined in terms of people who chose to come here as well as people who sought refuge here creates a dissonance with the much narrower discourse being developed in the public forums of government talk and the media. Australia is so mixed in its cultural composition that trying to define the 'us' within the Australian population is not so straightforward. We may indeed have reached a point of no return. The tension created by the inconsistency of the cultural imperative of lived experience and the dominant discourse provides an opportunity to seriously consider who 'we' are.

Australians are poised at a point in our history that might rightly be described as a defining moment - in which we need to clearly and thoughtfully consider what it means to be Australian. To define ourselves either solely in terms of what we have and must retain, or in terms of what we are able to contribute, must form part of the decision we need to make. The voices of young people may provide direction for the way in which this issue could be resolved. As one young Australian commented:

'helping someone makes you feel good at the end of the day. To say to yourself, 'I did something – I helped this person, this group', you feel happy. Whereas when you don't help them and just avoid them, you're going to have something empty, always, inside'.

By fencing out the 'other' needy, desperate, destitute who were seeking asylum on our shores we have created an 'us' who we now struggle to define. Let us do this defining in a spirit of openness and vision, rather than out of fear and mean spirited self-satisfaction. Let us not become prisoners of our own fence building.

REFERENCES

Badham, V. (2002) Young people and refugees. Streetwise Communications unpublished research.

BBC News, (2002), 'Australia unmoved by migrants' strike', 20 Jan 2002, http://news.bbc.co.uk/1/hi/world/asia-pacific/1769835.stm

Clennell, A. & Crichton, S. (2001) 'They're intimidating us: PM', *Sydney Morning Herald*, 29 Aug 2001.

Cornford, P. & Grattan, M. (2001), 'Children overboard, but boat in limbo on refugee frontline', *Sydney Morning Herald*, 8 Oct 2001, p. 1.

Hopkins, A. (2002), 'Australia 'regrets' false asylum seeker claims', Reuters, 28 Feb 2002.

Koutsoukis, J. (2004), 'Latham tackles multiculturalism', *The Age*, 21 April 2004, p. 1.

Orphant, M. (2001), 'Australia warns Illegals of Perils of Migration', Reuters, 26 Jan 2001.

Robbin, A. (2000), 'Classifying racial and ethnic group data in the United States; the politics of negotiation and accommodation', *Journal of Government Information*, 26(5), 467-83.

Skehan, C. (2004), 'Vanstone urged to release more asylum seekers', *Sydney Morning Herald*, 18 May 2004, p. 6.

Sydney Morning Herald (2002), 'Lipsewing', 21 Jan 2002, 10.

Taylor, K. (2001), 'Boat People warning just a 'draft', *The Age*, 11 Jan 2001.

van Dijk, T.A. (1987), *Communicating Racism. Ethnic Prejudice in Thought and Talk*. Sage Publications: London.

CHAPTER NINE
AN AFTERWORD

CHRIS SIDOTI

A year and a half has passed since the University of Western Sydney seminar at which these papers were delivered. I am writing this afterword two years to the day after the Tampa Affair. Much has changed in that time. The injustice done to refugees and asylum seekers has not ended. It has not gone away, even though political and media attention moved on long ago to other issues – the War against Terrorism, the War against Iraq, the possible War against North Korea, the Military Intervention in the Solomon Islands. There is so much talk of war and violence that the Australian Government's continuing injustice towards refugees and asylum seekers cannot draw more than passing comment. A bit like the situation of indigenous people in Australia actually.

The injustice has not gone away over the last two years but its nature has changed fundamentally.

Changes since 2001

First, over the past three years only one boat of asylum seekers has come to Australia, towards the middle of 2003. That boat came from Vietnam and was allegedly arranged by a Vietnamese Australian who was so distressed and frustrated by the Australian Government's refusal to permit his family to join him here that he decided to risk all on this boat trip. Of course he is now considered a people smuggler and is in custody awaiting criminal trial. But no other boats have come. The overthrow of the Taliban regime in Afghanistan and of Saddam Hussein in Iraq and the Australian Government's policy of interdiction off shore have succeeded in stopping the boats, at least for now. This is a good thing. The crossing from Indonesia to Australia in these leaking, over-crowded boats is an inherently dangerous practice that cost at least 355 lives in October and November 2001 alone.

Second, the end of the boats has meant that the numbers of boat people in detention centres have declined and that those still detained are there awaiting deportation. In August 2001 there were 3721 people in the Australian camps. In August 2003 there are around 1200, of whom fewer than 600 are boat people. The number of detainees then has been reduced by two thirds. The Curtin and Woomera camps have been closed; the new camp at Baxter has been opened. All boat people have had initial decisions on their applications for asylum and almost all have exhausted all review processes. So the nature of the detention centre population has changed. It is no longer made up of asylum seekers but of rejected applicants for protection awaiting deportation. The problem is that most have no realistic prospect of being deported in the reasonably foreseeable future.

Third, the introduction of the temporary visa scheme in 1999 and its extension in 2001 has left almost 9000 refugees in Australia without security of protection and residence, without adequate support to live and work in Australian and, most serious of all, without their families. The first 2200 of these visas have or are about to expire and those with the visas are awaiting decisions on their immediate fates. They fear being sent back to inherently dangerous and unstable situations in Afghanistan and Iraq. They are understandably deeply distressed – traumatised not only by persecution and flight, but by lengthy detention in Australia and now isolation and insecurity.

Priorities to Address Injustice

The changes that have occurred over the past three years pose new questions and require new priorities to address the human rights of asylum seekers. There are five issues now requiring priority attention.

First, what is to be done with *non-deportable deportees*? Almost all the boat people in detention now are not asylum seekers awaiting determination of their claims for protection but rejected applicants awaiting deportation. The problem is that most have no realistic prospect of being deported any time in the foreseeable future.

Most prospective deportees are Afghani or Iraqi. The new Afghanistan Government is struggling to reintegrate the hundreds of thousands of refugees who have already returned from camps in Iran and Pakistan. It has indicated that it is willing to accept those who return

136

voluntarily but not at this stage any forced returnees. The United Nations High Commissioner for Refugees has agreed with the Afghani Government's position on returnees. The United States' occupation authority in Iraq has given no indication that it has the capacity at this stage to receive back any of the hundreds of thousands who have fled that country. The continuing, indeed increasing, violence there causes concern that it may be many years before asylum seekers can return in safety and be re-integrated successfully.

Neither the Government nor the Opposition has been prepared to discuss this issue. It did not rate even a mention in the Labor policy released in 2002. Does this need to be updated? The courts have not been as reluctant as the major political parties to deal with this issue. In 2002 the Federal Court ordered the release of a Palestinian detainee awaiting deportation. It held that his continued detention was unlawful because there was no prospect of his deportation in the foreseeable future. Other similar challenges were made and the Australian Government sought to overturn the original decisions. Ultimately the High Court rejected the Government's appeal. The law therefore requires the release of persons awaiting deportation if there is no realistic prospect of deportation being effected within a reasonable time. The Family Court too has shown leadership in asserting jurisdiction in relation to children in detention. It has begun to order their release on the basis of their best interests. This approach is also being challenged by the Government in the High Court.

These initiatives by the courts, however, will not be the end of the matter. Over the past decade Australian Governments of both political persuasions have rushed to change immigration law whenever the High Court has decided a case against their wishes. The present Government has said it will try to do now as it has done in the past. Whether it succeeds again in changing the law in these circumstances, however, is another matter now that bipartisanship on immigration detention policy has ended.

The situation of non-deportable deportees is an urgent humanitarian issue that needs to be resolved more satisfactorily than the current practice. I do not argue that Australia is required to permit unauthorised arrivals who are not refugees to stay. There is no basis in international human rights law that would support such an argument. But they should not be detained indefinitely until circumstances change to permit their deportation. Only those who have committed a crime under Australian law and been sentenced to imprisonment by an Australian court require detention. The others, the great majority, have committed no crime and their continued detention is unreasonable and inhumane. Although temporary protection visas are inappropriate for refugees they could be used quite appropriately to permit the release of persons awaiting deportation who are unlikely to be able to be deported within a short time.

The second priority is *improving conditions in the immigration detention centres*. I accept the difficulty of establishing and maintaining the best possible conditions in camps when they are over-crowded and have to integrate large numbers of new people. Now that there has been only one new boat in three years, there are few new people and the camps are no longer over-crowded. Now we should expect that those detained will enjoy conditions that are as good as possible. Detainees are not criminal offenders and they should be treated better than criminals. In fact their conditions of detention are far worse than in the worst Australian prisons.

The new camp at Baxter was opened in 2002. It has been described as state of the art but, from what I have heard, it is better described as an electronic zoo. I remember when Katingal Prison was opened in New South Wales many years ago. It too was described both as state of the art and as an electronic zoo. It was a very modern, high tech prison with the latest in surveillance and control equipment. From the very beginning it was a nightmare to manage. After constant destructive action by inmates and a series of riots an independent inquiry recommended that it be closed as inhumane, degrading and unusable. It was. I fear that the Katingal experience has been forgotten, that the designers of Baxter have made the same mistakes. Time will tell. Conditions in detention must be improved.

Third, there is urgent need and now a good opportunity to *change the refugee determination process*. The current process is not good enough. It gets it wrong too many times. In 2001-02 the Refugee Review Tribunal upheld the appeals of 62% of rejected Afghani applicants and 87% of rejected Iraqi applicants. Of all applications heard by the Tribunal it set aside 44% of negative decisions affecting people in detention. Departmental decision makers got it wrong many times. And then when the Federal Court heard applications for review of Refugee Review Tribunal decisions, it set aside 18.2% of those decisions. The Tribunal too got it wrong many times. There is a clear need for a truly independent process of determination and for supervision and review by higher administrative tribunals and courts.

To begin with, as the Human Rights and Equal Opportunity Commission recommended in 1998, the refugee determination function should be removed from the immigration department. That department was established a century ago to control immigration to Australia. Controlling immigration is part of each country's sovereign right to determine who is or is not permitted to enter and remain within that country. General immigration is a discretionary issue that can be regulated and enforced. Refugee determination is an exception, however. Countries that have ratified the refugee treaties, which Australia has, have binding legal obligations to accept and protect refugees within their jurisdiction. Proper determination of refugee status is a legal obligation not an immigration discretion. It should be entrusted to a legal agency, not to public servants, and it should fall within the responsibility of the Attorney General, not the immigration minister and department.

The process should also incorporate proper administrative and judicial review to ensure the accuracy and lawfulness of determinations. The excision of Australian territory from the migration zone has excluded many refugee determination decisions from administrative review by the Refugee Review Tribunal. The limitations on judicial review and the widespread use of privative clauses in refugee law have eliminated almost any opportunity for judicial review. These changes to the determination process are unreasonable and, at a pragmatic level, unnecessary. They were introduced to overcome perceived abuse of the system but no abuse was ever shown. On the contrary what was demonstrated year after year was that original bureaucratic decision makers got it wrong far too often and that even the expert review panel got it wrong at times. Experience shows that proper review is essential, not that it is abusive. Understandable concerns about the time taken for the review processes and the costs involved should have been addressed by ensuring adequate resources for the tribunal and court to undertake the reviews promptly and procedural changes to streamline the process.

Critics of the present system have worked hard to develop an excellent alternative to the system of indefinite mandatory detention of asylum seekers. The priority now is for the same hard work to be done to develop an alternative processing system that meets the requirements of human rights, natural justice, accuracy and efficiency. The present system is unacceptable in principle and a failure in fact.

Fourth, the *temporary protection visa system* should be abandoned for recognised refugees. It traumatises those subject to the scheme by subjecting them to continued insecurity. I have already discussed that.

In addition to these humanitarian considerations the policy is simply not in Australia's interests. Until temporary protection visas were introduced in 1999, Australian Governments since federation had been committed to permanent settlement of immigrants. They explicitly did not want significant numbers of short-term migrant workers and still do not. They sought permanent commitment from those who came across the seas seeking new lives in this country so that the newcomers would become part of the Australian community, throwing in their lots with the rest of us for mutual advancement. All that changed in October 1999. Now we have people here for periods of years who are insecure, traumatised, denied assistance to learn English, accorded a discriminatory status that inhibits their integration into the broader community, left unsupported by and worried about their spouses and children. Self evidently this is not in Australia's interests.

The priority in changing the temporary visa system is to permit family reunion. The forced separation of families even for a period of three years, which is Labor policy, is unacceptable. Indefinite separation through a series of rolling temporary visas, which is the Government policy, is intolerable. Recognised refugees should be entitled to bring to Australia their spouses, their children and, where they have dependent parents, then those parents too. This is not "opening the floodgates" to uncontrolled migration of large numbers of people. It is simply a humane way to permit those closest and most dependent family members to be re-united in this country.

Finally priority should be given to better responses to *refugee needs outside Australia*. One of the factors that have contributed to stopping the flow of boats has been a greater commitment to action further back along the line of refugee movement. Stronger regional cooperation to stop people smuggling has been the principal focus of Australian Government activity but it should be only one element of a better, more integrated response that prevents the need for refugee movement in the first place.

The conditions of refugees in the countries to which they first flee are often harsh. Often they are subjected to persecution and

140

discrimination once again. They are often denied legal status and protection. They can be accommodated in camps in the most appalling conditions. They often have little choice but to move on, to seek protection elsewhere, in countries further away, like Australia. Australia should apply all its diplomatic and political skill towards ensuring that refugees are received and treated properly and their human rights are respected in the countries to which they first flee. It should put dollars behind this effort, increasing its financial support for the United Nations High Commissioner for Refugees, which manages the camps, beyond a token amount to something substantial. It should also increase its own refugee intake from the camps so that refugees have a real prospect of orderly re-settlement and do not feel the same pressure to move on through unsafe, unorthodox means.

The best way to resolve refugee problems, of course, is to prevent the circumstances that force people to flee in the first place. People do not become refugees by choice. They are driven from their homes by situations beyond their control: persecution and war. There are more refugees now than ever before, the result of a decade of genocide, human rights violations and violence. Only enhanced international efforts by the United Nations and the international community generally will promote effective resolution of present refugee problems and the prevention of new ones. Australia should give high priority to preventive work, addressing the causes of refugee flows and not merely the consequences. That will require not only greater efforts by Australian Governments but greater awareness, understanding and commitment by the Australian people.

Too often, unfortunately, we have been taken by surprise by developments even in our own region, unaware of what has been happening and ignorant of the historical, political and cultural contexts in which events occur. We require a serious commitment to educating Australians about our region. We need to demonstrate political and financial commitment to the well-being of our near and not so near neighbours. As we learned painfully through the Bali bombing, events in our region and the wider world can have a profound effect on us. We need to anticipate events and not merely react to them.

Conclusion

The issues have changed but the injustice has not gone away. It will not go away until it is addressed properly. Australia has the opportunity now, when there are no boats and so no pressures on the system, to fix it up. Those who are trapped in the present system, as non-deportable detainees or as refugees offered only temporary protection without their families, deserve better, more just treatment. Without doubt, one day the boats will start coming again. Those who will come on those boats deserve far better treatment than that accorded past arrivals. Now we have the opportunity to fix it up for present and future asylum seekers. What has not changed is the intransigence of the Australian Government in the face of great human need. Nor has there been much change in the enthusiasm with which large numbers of our fellow Australians support it. Changing that remains our greatest challenge.

.